Contents

Dedicated to my father, Dr. V.K. Ranjan for instilling the value of continuous learning and sharing knowledge.

Dad, your passion for reading and teaching has been my best source of inspiration.

Thank You!

Foreword

Enterprises today are looking for agility and maturity in their IT environment for two reasons; one, globalization and digitization make the technology more critical than ever before and IT capability becomes the competitive differentiator and two, latest technology such as cloud and social computing unleash the potential to decentralize the IT and democratize the information. It is extremely important that students and professionals, who are aspiring for enterprise software development career, learn how to architect design and develop new breed of application.

BigData is bringing big risks and big challenges to the enterprise; data management solutions such as data storage, data quality, MDM, data integration, data security and governance. These are one of the top priorities for business and IT department to focus on, to breakdown the department silo, let the data flow cross the border, and keep organizational data asset both safe and clean with holistic view.

Information management and BigData are my passion and I see every day working with customers that scarce resource in these highly skilled areas of software engineering is hindering business's ability to leverage these technologies and gain competitive advantage.

Recognizing the need for such skills, I find this book extremely relevant to the students of software engineering discipline. Rakesh has put together his years of software engineering and client experience to create this textbook and I hope you will find it useful for your course work and beyond when you work on solving enterprise IT problems.

Thank you and enjoy the book.

Kaushik Bhaskar

Director of Information Management

IBM Corporation

Acknowledgements

I had a privilege of writing two books with some of my distinguished colleagues before. Those two books were focused on specific products and technologies. This is my first attempt to write solo on a topic that is too vast and dynamic. As always, I want to thank my family for their support and understanding along the way.

Personally, this book is for my two little angels: Rashi and Maansi. They are a true joy to be around and are the best thing that ever happened in my life. Rashi has helped me with the sketches for this book (thanks to free AutoCAD Sketchbook app for iPad). Thank you dear, I love you! My wife Mausami played an important role of critically reviewing (specially Big Data topics) and proof reading the book, Thank you.

Professionally, I want to thank a lot of my colleagues and great managers who I have worked with, specially my mentors Bala Iyer (In loving memory) and Prof. Dan Harkey.

I also want to thank my students Medha Srinivasarao, Krunal Vora and Harnika Sahni for testing chapter exercises and providing valuable input to this book.

-Rakesh Ranjan

ENTERPRISE SOFTWARE PLATFORM

A Textbook for Software Engineering Students

Enterprise Software

Platform

Chapter

1

Introduction to Enterprise Software Platform

Chapter Goal

After studying this chapter, you should be able to:

- Understand the architecture overview of a software development platform and its core components.
- Understand the various terminologies used in the context of enterprise software and systems.

Introduction

Enterprise Software Systems are software applications that automate and integrate all or many of the key business processes (workflow, messaging and services) of an organization. The term enterprise refers to an organization of individuals or entities, presumably working together to achieve some common goals. Organizations come in all shapes and sizes, large and small, for-profit and nonprofit, governmental and nongovernmental. Chances are, however, that when someone uses the term enterprise, they mean a large, for-profit organization, such as IBM, General Electric, Wells Fargo or eBay. Enterprises generally have some common needs, such as information sharing and processing, asset management and tracking, resource planning, customer or client management, protection of intellectual property, and so on. The term enterprise software is used to collectively refer to all software involved in supporting these common elements of an enterprise. Sketch 1-1 depicts typical architecture overview of an enterprise software system. Software is organized along the various functions within the organization, for example, sales, human resources, and so on. A firewall is provided to safeguard enterprise data from unauthorized access. Some software systems such as those for sales and inventory management interact; however, most are fairly isolated piece of software.

Enterprise software may consist of a multitude of distinct pieces today, but enterprises have gradually come to realize that there is a strong need for their diverse systems to integrate well and leverage each other wherever appropriate for maximum enterprise benefit. Business-to-Business (B2B) and Business to Commerce (B2C) are good examples of such integration.

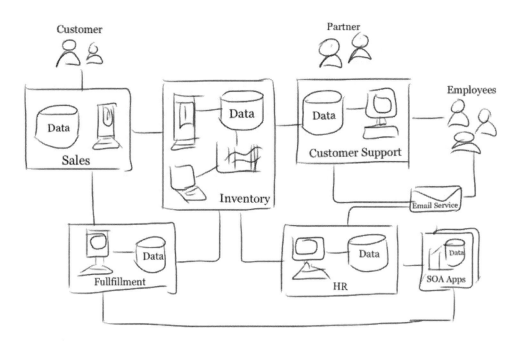

Sketch 1.1   Enterprise Software Systems Overview

As a result of the renewed focus on enterprise application integration, the term integrated software enterprise is emerging which envisions:

*   Integrating product knowledge and skills and offering it as a service on web to provide better services and support to customers.

- Connecting traditional marketing to social media to develop enterprise wide marketing strategy to reach out to broader audience.
- Creating service oriented architecture to integrate vendors, suppliers and partners to create new business opportunity and fuel growth in untapped market.
- Developing enterprise wide tools for managing human resources and their skills, enabling business processes such as 401K, and employee benefits management as a service.
- Developing information management strategy to unlock the vast amount of structured and unstructured information for business insight.

Challenges in developing and managing enterprise software?

Successful enterprises tend to grow in size, hire more people, have more customers and more web site hits, have bigger sales and revenues, add more locations, and so on. In order to support this growth, enterprise software must be scalable in terms of accommodating a larger enterprise and its operations.

Enterprises encounter constraints as they grow. One common constraint is the computer hardware's inability to scale as the enterprise's processing needs increase. Another constraint is the enterprise's ability to put more people in the same physical or geographical location. Thus, the challenge of distribution comes into the picture. Multiple physical machines solve the processing needs but introduce the challenges of distributed software. New building or geographical locations address the immediate need, but they introduce the challenge of bringing the same level of services to a diversely located enterprise. Connecting previously separate systems in order to gain enterprise-scale efficiencies can be a major challenge. Legacy systems were typically designed with specific purposes in mind and were not specifically conceived with integration with other systems in mind.

Enterprise software also typically requires some common capabilities, such as security services to safeguard the enterprise knowledge, transaction services to guarantee integrity of data, and so on. Each of these requires specific skills and knowledge. For instance, proper transaction handling requires strategies for recovering from failures, handling multiuser situations, ensuring consistency across transactions, and so on. Similarly, implementing security might demand a grasp of various security protocols and security management approaches. These are just some of the common challenges that must be addressed when dealing with enterprise software development.

Enterprise Software Delivery Model

With emergence of Software as a Service, the way we used to design, develop, build and deploy software is changing. The sketch below depicts vendor side activities and consumer side activities involved from the stage of building the software to the stage of consuming the software. Vendors no more have to ship software on a physical or electronic media if software is being made available as a service. This is eliminating several activities including operation and maintenance of software systems on part of customers. Customers are able to focus on their core business and not bogged down on complicated IT issues. This trend is going to continue and more and more vendors will be offering their software products as a service. Cloud computing and virtualization being at the core of SaaS, new programming and deployment models are emerging in the cloud area. As a future software architect, you need to learn the cloud computing programming models and architecture of the components, which make software working on the cloud. You will also need to learn the emerging security and storage architecture that applies to various characteristics of SaaS including multi-tenancy.

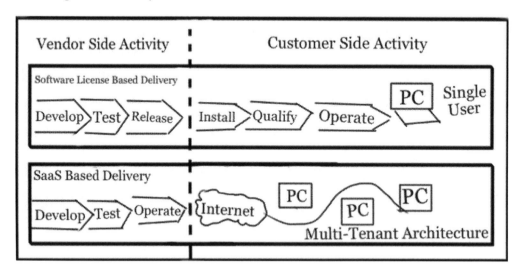

Sketch 1.2 Software Delivery Model

Software Licensing Model

Evolution of Open Source Software has put huge pressure on commercial software vendors and has forced them to change their software licensing model over the past few years. Vendors are moving from traditional licensing model where client had fixed access to software either with named or shared license with limitation on how long they can access to considerably flexible models where client can dictate how much they want to pay and how they want to use the software.

Cloud computing and "Software as a Service" have brought pay per use models which are great for customers who would like to use the software without having resources to install and maintain the software.

Open Source Software

Open source in Information Technology is software whose source code is published and made available to the public, enabling anyone to copy, modify and redistribute the source code without paying royalties or fees. Today there is open source software available as an alternative to pretty much every government and enterprise software needs. The following table shows some prominent open source software that can be chosen as viable alternative to save cost and licensing fees. Please note that in some cases, comparison may not be fair as the open source alternatives may not offer all the bells and whistles that their commercial counterpart do, but most of them offer a layered based architecture where a business can start small with core feature set and buy advanced features and services when they grow.

Application Servers

Open Source	Compared to	Resource link
Apache Tomcat	IBM Websphere	http://tomcat.apache.org/
Redhat JBoss	Oracle Weblogic	http://www.jboss.org/
Oracle Glassfish		https://glassfish.java.net/
Apache Geronimo		http://geronimo.apache.org/

Middleware Software

Open Source	Compared to	Resource link
RabbitMQ	IBM MQ	http://www.rabbitmq.com/
JBoss	Oracle Weblogic	http://www.jboss.org/

Talend http://www.talend.com/

Cloud Computing Software

Open Source	Compared to	Resource link
Open Stack	Amazon Web Service	http://www.openstack.org/
Eucalyptus	Microsoft Azure	http://www.eucalyptus.com/
OpenNebula	VMWare	http://opennebula.org/
	Citrix	

Relational Database Software

Open Source	Compared to	Resource link
MySQL	IBM DB2	http://www.mysql.com/
PostgreSQL	Oracle	http://www.postgresql.org/
	MS SQL Server	

Code Repository and Version Control

Open Source	Compared to	Resource link
Git, Subversion	Rational Team	http://git-scm.com/
	Sourcesafe	http://subversion.apache.org/
	Perforce	

Enterprise Resource Planning (ERP)

Open Source	Compared to	Resource link
OpenERP	SAP, Oracle	https://www.openerp.com/
OpenBravo	Microsoft Dynamics	http://www.openbravo.com/

Customer Relationship Management (CRM)

Open Source	Compared to	Resource link
SugarCRM	Salesforce	http://www.sugarcrm.com/
	Microsoft Dynamics	

Enterprise Records Management

Open Source	Compared to	Resource link
Alfresco	Microsoft Sharepoint	http://www.alfresco.com/
	Documentum	

Business Intelligence Software

Open Source	Compared to	Resource link
Pentaho BI	Oracle, IBM	http://www.pentaho.com/

Informatica

Desktop Operating System

Open Source	Compared to	Resource link
Redhat Fedora	Microsoft Windows	http://fedoraproject.org/
OpenSuse	XP, 7, 8	http://www.opensuse.org/en/
Ubuntu		

Evolution of Software Platform

A software platform is nothing but accumulation of computing technologies developed over the decades. It is a framework and provides foundation for software and applications to be developed. Until 1990, mainframe ruled the world and all software systems were tied to these systems. The advantages of mainframe were many; centralized system offered simplicity, security and colocation of resources. Some of the disadvantages included extremely expensive hardware and software, single point of failure, limited accessibility and limited choices of programming languages to develop applications.

Such centralized systems are called Single Tier software application. In software, tier is an abstraction, which helps us understand the architecture by breaking down the system in logical components. From application point of view, single tier system posed the challenge in which, presentation, data and business logic were intermingled together. Any changes to one of these layers would cause a ripple effect on other layers and break the application. Another disadvantage of this interdependency was the limitations it imposed on reuse of business logic or other data components.

In 1990s, client server model was picking up which alleviated the problem by moving the presentation and business logic to a different tier. However, the presentation and business logic layer remain intermingled which still caused the same problem. Data layer was separated but applications were still vulnerable to break when data update happened in a distributed environment.

The n-tier approach attempted to fix this problem by separating these components for reuse and robustness. The important point to note here are that these n-tier applications may not necessarily require separate piece of hardware; although that is certainly possible.

What does a Software platform consists of?

A software platform may consist of the following or more:

- Programming techniques such as Object Oriented, Functional, Scripting, Framework based, Hadoop, MapReduce
- Tools and Interfaces
- Interface languages such as Interface Definition Language (IDL), Web Services Description Language (WSDL), Simplified Wrapper and Interface Generator (SWIG)
- Communication protocols such as TCPIP, Distributed/Network services
- Middleware for Transaction processing, Analytic platform
- Run time components
- OS platforms such as Linux
- New layer is always added

Java as a Software Platform

Java was started as a programming language and quickly became a choice of millions of programmers around the world. Since its inception, Java has grown big and evolved as a software platform because more and more layers have been added to the language itself. As a result, Java as a software platform offers everything to develop an enterprise-ready networked application. The libraries and toolkits that have been added as layers are all standard based; hence providing a great deal of portability and flexibility along all hardware platforms. This makes software integration easy within the enterprise.

Brief History of Java

- 1993 Oak project at Sun
  - small, robust, architecture independent, Object-Oriented, language to control interactive TV.
  - didn't go anywhere
- 1995 Oak becomes Java
  - Focus on the web
- 1996 Java 1.0 available

- 1997 (March) Java 1.1 - some language changes, much larger library, new event handling model
- 1997 (September) Java 1.2 beta – huge increase in libraries including Swing, new collection classes, J2EE
- 1998 (October) Java 1.2 final (Java2!)
- 2000 (April) Java 1.3 final
- 2001 Java 1.4 final (assert)
- 2004 Java 1.5 (parameterized types, enum) (Java5!)
- 2005 J2EE 1.5
- 2006 (December) Java 1.6 (Quick starter, place-in-place, security fixes)
- 2011 (July) Java SE 7 (JDK for ARM, JavaFX enhancement for touch)

Service Oriented Architecture (SOA)

SOA is an approach to IT that builds business processes from reusable component modules or services that are independent of applications and the computing platforms on which they run. Software assets become building blocks that can be reused in developing other applications.

- Focus is on application assembly rather than implementation details
- Can be used internally to create new applications out of existing components
- Can be used externally to integrate with applications outside of the enterprise

SOA means different things to different people. For a **business user**, SOA is a set of capabilities that a business wants to expose as services to its clients and partners. The examples are making services such as Pension and 401K available to employees.

For a **system architect**, SOA is an architectural style, which requires a service provider, requestor and a service description. It addresses characteristics such as reuse, loose coupling and simple implementation.

For a **software system implementer**, SOA is a programming model, which includes standards, tools, methods and technologies such as web services.

System Architect = above the Code who understands how all of the software works together

And finally for an **operation person**, SOA is a set of agreements between service consumers and service providers that specify the quality of service (QoS) and identify key business and metrics.

Adoption of cloud computing in enterprise

Changing IT roles in procurement and providing software and systems is driving adoption of cloud computing in enterprises today. Evolution of cloud computing and software as a service is empowering business users. These users are making their own decisions on what software to buy and use to develop their business solutions. Democratization of enterprise data is helping them. Internet of things (IoT) is fuelling the cloud computing market. Big data analytics is another influencer. More and more businesses are becoming software companies. Think about all these Blood glucose monitors becoming wifi enabled sending your daily blood sugar report to the cloud which can be consumed by your medical record application. As business applications are becoming more central to business offerings, application developers who create these application become more important. Developers drove the early growth of cloud computing and they are now influencing IT purchase decisions fuelling more growth in cloud services. Security and privacy concerns around cloud will drive private cloud growth. Vision of hybrid cloud will become reality where cloud will be treated as a single homogeneous technology spanning internal data centers and external cloud services. Platform as a service offering by major software vendor is going to drive cloud computing adoption in big enterprises as it will help application developers bringing new applications to market quickly and inexpensively. The PaaS model is discussed in detail in Cloud computing chapter.

* Big Companies can have Procurement departments who are in charge of buying

Operating System Overview

Chapter Goal

After studying this chapter, you should be able to:

- Refresh your operating system knowledge that will be useful in understanding subsequent topics in the book
- Learn some of the distinguished features of Linux operating system useful for understanding middleware and distributed software concepts

Introduction to the Operating System

An operating system Abstracts the real hardware of the system and presents the system's users and its applications with a virtual machine. Some of the major responsibilities of an operating system include:

- Handling input output (I/O) to and from attached hardware devices
- Managing file I/O
- Supporting different file systems
- Managing all other programs running on the computer (determines which applications should run, in what order and determines the time slice of a process)
- Managing sharing of the internal memory among multiple applications

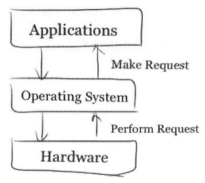

Sketch 2.1 A simple version of operating system

A Brief History of UNIX Operating System

UNIX was developed in the late 1960s; researchers from General Electric, MIT and Bell Labs launched a joint project to develop an ambitious multi-user, multi-tasking OS for mainframe computers known as MULTICS (Multiplexed Information and Computing System). The MULTICS project did not succeed, but it did inspire Ken Thompson, who was a researcher at Bell Labs, to write a simpler operating system himself. He wrote a simpler version of MULTICS on a PDP7 in assembler and called his attempt UNICS (Uniplexed Information and Computing System). Because memory and CPU power were at a premium in those days, UNICS (eventually shortened to UNIX) used short commands to minimize the space needed to store them and the time needed to decode them - hence the tradition of short UNIX commands we use today, e.g. ls, cp, rm, mv etc.

Ken Thompson then teamed up with Dennis Ritchie, the author of the first C compiler in 1973. They rewrote the UNIX kernel in C that was a big step forwards in terms of the system's portability and released the Fifth Edition of UNIX to universities in 1974. The Seventh Edition, released in 1978, marked a split in UNIX development into two main branches: SYSV (System 5) and BSD (Berkeley Software Distribution). BSD arose from the UC Berkeley where Thompson spent a sabbatical year. Students at Berkeley and other research institutions continued its development. AT&T and other commercial companies developed SYSV.

The UNIX Family Tree

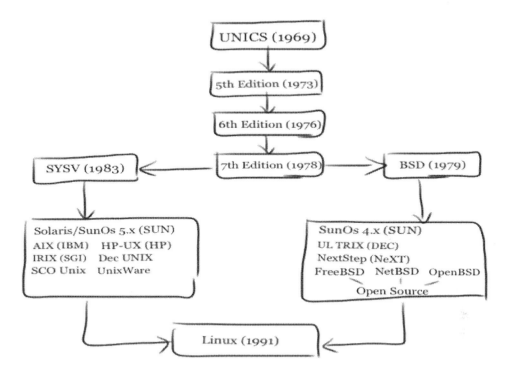

Sketch 2.2 UNIX Operating System Family Tree

Linux Kernel Subsystem

The kernel is the "core" of any computer system; it is the software, which allows users to share computer resources. It is responsible for interfacing all of your applications that are running in "user mode" down to the physical hardware, and allowing processes, known as servers, to get information from each other using inter-process communication (IPC).

With over 13 million lines of code, Linux kernel is one of the largest open source project in the world. In general most of the kernel software falls into one of the three categories: monolithic, microkernel and hybrid. While Linux kernel is a monolithic one, OS X and Windows 7 use hybrid kernels.

Microkernels

Microkernels are commonly used in embedded applications. The idea is simple: manage only that it has to – CPU, memory and Inter process communication (IPC). Everything else in the computer is handled as separate accessory and work in user mode. Microkernels are portable and secure. They have very small footprint both in size and memory usage. The main drawbacks of microkernels are that device drivers run in non-privileged mode hence run slower.

Monolithic kernels

Monolithic kernels are opposite of microkernels because they don't just manage CPU, memory and IPC but they also manage file systems, device drivers, network interfaces and system calls. Monolithic kernels are proven to be better at accessing hardware and multi-tasking because if a program has to get data from memory or another process, it has a direct way to get them.

The figure below shows various components of a Linux kernel subsystem.

- Normal programs execute in user mode
- Kernel programs execute in kernel mode (privileged mode)
- Kernel takes requests from applications running in user mode and performs requested operations on the hardware.
- Linux kernel consists of several important parts: process management, memory management, hardware device drivers, file system drivers, network management and various other bits and pieces.

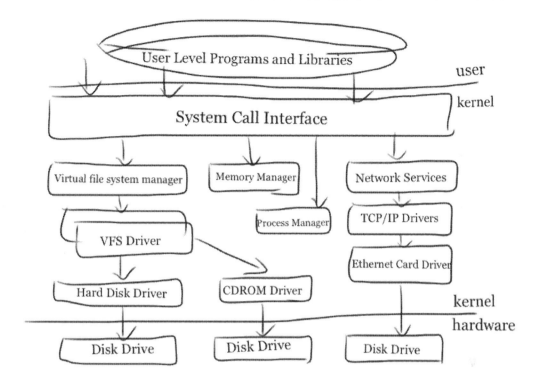

Sketch 2.3 Detailed version of Linux Operating System

Because Linux kernel is monolithic, it has largest footprint and the most complexity over the other types of kernels. But the good thing Linux kernel developers have done is that they made kernel modules separated so that they can be loaded at run time. This allows user to load desired kernel module on the fly. Because of this modular nature you can easily customize your kernel by setting modules to load or not load during startup/boot process. Linux kernel source code can be found and browsed at https://www.kernel.org/

Hybrid Kernels

Hybrid kernels are most versatile ones because they have ability to pick and choose what they want to run in user mode and what they want to run in privileged mode. Usually device drivers and file system access will be run in user mode and system calls and IPC will run in privileged mode. This provides flexibility but different add-on hardware manufacturers have responsibility to test and provide drivers for the kernel.

What's so special about Linux?

Linux today runs on pretty much everything:

- Embedded devices
- Laptops and desktops
- Small and large servers
- Mega clusters and super computers

As devices are re-sculpted for wireless networking, IPv6 Internet access, and touchscreen interfaces, real-time operating systems continue to be replaced by more advanced embedded operating systems like Linux Embedded. The current trend is that Linux is making headways in just about all embedded categories, including automotive, home automation, retail, industrial, medical and digital imaging.

Most Linux software including Linux kernel are available under GPL (GNU Public License), which means:

- You can copy the software
- You get the source code
- You can alter the source code and recompile it
- You can distribute altered source and binaries
- You can charge money for all this

But, you can't change the license, which means:

- All your customers have the same rights as you
- So you really can't make money from selling the software alone

Linux Boot Process

1. CPU Initialization
2. Execute single instruction and jump to BIOS (ROM)
3. BIOS finds boot device and fetches MBR(on the hard disk/CDROM/or any registered devices)
4. MBR points to LILO(Linux Loader/boot manager, similar to windows boot.ini)
5. LILO loads compressed Linux kernel
6. Compressed kernel is decompressed and loaded

7. Root file system mounted
8. Init (mother of all processes) process started
9. Rest is all forking of new processes (kernel remains uncompressed in protected mode)

Linux Process Overview

A program or a command that is actually running on a system is referred to as a process. Linux can run a number of different commands at the same time as well as many occurrences of the same program (such as **vi**) at the same process. The Linux kernel holds an internal table, called the process table, in which the information about running processes is kept. A shell is a special process that is able to read user commands and can start the appropriate program. One of the built-in commands of the shell is **echo**, which displays something on the screen, and one of the built-in shell variables is **$$**, which displays the Process ID (PID) of the shell. Each process has its own environment:

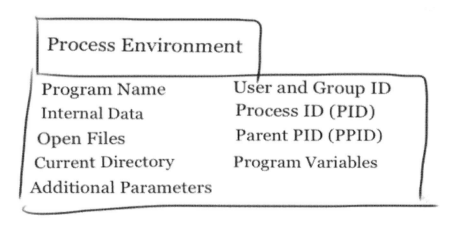

Sketch 2.4 Linux Process Environment

Starting and Stopping of a Process

All processes in a Linux system are started by another process, so for each and every process you can identify the parent (the process that started this particular process) and the children (the processes that were started by this particular process), if any. There is one exception to this. The **init** process is started by the kernel itself, and always has Process ID 11. Processes do not run forever. They can be terminated because of two reasons; because the process terminates itself, either automatically (when the work has been done) or based on user input (such as a user entering "ZZ" in **vi**), or when another process sends a "signal" to the process.

Process Summary

A program is an executable stored somewhere (perhaps on hard disk) in a computer. This program owns no resources and cannot do anything until it gets executed. Once executed, a process is created which does own resources. Inside of this running process, threads can be used to do extra work for the process.

Life Cycle of a process

- Linux process is created using fork () and terminated either using exit () or by receiving a signal. Implementation is in kernel/fork.c and kernel/exit.c respectively.
- Processes communicate with each other (IPC) and with the kernel
- Linux supports IPCs such as signals and pipes
- Processes are protected from one another – kernel gives them separate address space.
- New processes (specially child threads) are created by cloning a currently running process using clone()

Managing Process Priorities

Processes on a Linux system are scheduled according to priority: When the CPU is free to run a process, it looks through the process table for a process with the lowest *priority number*. This process then gets a timeslice on the CPU. The priority number of a process is continuously changed. Three factors influence this:

- After a process has had a certain amount of CPU time, its priority number is increased, meaning that next time the CPU becomes available; the process is less likely to be first in the list.
- After a process has been idle (not using CPU time) for a while (either because it is waiting for something to happen, or because other processes are keeping the CPU busy), the priority number is decreased.
- The priority number can never become lower than the *nice value* that was set for that process. This scheme results in a usage pattern where every process with the same nice value gets an equal amount of CPU time.

Processes with a higher nice value get less CPU time than processes with a low nice value.

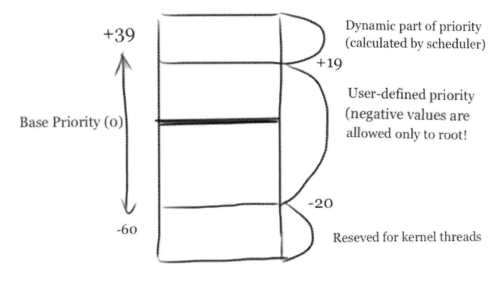

Sketch 2.5 Process Priorities

Memory Management

Virtual memory makes system appear to have more RAM than it really has. It allows sharing of RAM between competing processes as they need it. Hard drive space is used to extend physical memory. Virtual memory provides:

- Large address spaces (swapper, pagefile etc.)
- Protection (process has its own virtual address space)
- Memory mapping (image and data files are mapped into virtual address space)
- Fair physical memory allocation
- Shared virtual memory

Paging

Linux uses a technique called demand paging. Memory pages of a process are brought into RAM only when a process attempts to use them. Linux Kernel alters the process's page table marking the virtual areas as existing but not in memory. As there is much less physical memory than virtual memory the operating system must be careful that it does not use the physical memory inefficiently. One way to save physical memory is to only load virtual pages that are currently being used by the executing program. For example, a database program may be run to query a database. In this case, not the entire database needs to be loaded into memory, just those data records that are being examined. If the database query is a search query then it does not make sense to load the code from the database program that deals with adding new records. This technique of only loading virtual pages into memory as they are accessed is known as demand paging.

Page Fault

When a process X attempts to access a virtual address that is not currently in memory the processor cannot find a page table entry for the virtual page referenced. so if process X attempts to read from an address within virtual page frame number the processor cannot translate the address into a physical one. At this point the processor notifies the operating system that a page fault has occurred.

If the faulting virtual address is invalid this means that the process has attempted to access a virtual address that it should not have. Maybe the application has gone wrong in some way, for example writing to random addresses in memory. In this case the operating system will terminate it, protecting the other processes in the system from this rogue process.

If the faulting virtual address was valid but the page that it refers to is not currently in memory, the operating system must bring the appropriate page into memory from the image on disk. Disk access takes a long time, relatively speaking, and so the process must wait quite a while until the page has been fetched. If there are other processes that could run then the operating system will select one of them to run. The fetched page is written into a free physical page frame and an entry for the virtual page frame number is added to the processes page table. The process is then restarted at the machine instruction where the memory fault occurred. This time the virtual memory access is made, the processor can make the virtual to physical address translation and so the process continues to run.

Swapping

If a process needs to bring a virtual page into physical memory and there are no free physical pages available, the operating system must make room for this page by discarding another page from physical memory. If the page to be discarded from physical memory came from an image or data file and has not been written to then the page does not need to be saved. Instead it can be discarded and if the process needs that page again it can be brought back into memory from the image or data file.

However, if the page has been modified, the operating system must preserve the contents of that page so that it can be accessed at a later time. This type of page is known as a **dirty page** and when it is removed from memory it is saved in a special file called the **swap file**. Accesses to the swap file are very long relative to the speed of the processor and physical memory and the operating system must juggle the need to write pages to disk with the need to retain them in memory to be used again.

If the algorithm used to decide which pages to discard or swap (the *swap algorithm* is not efficient then a condition known as *thrashing* occurs. In this case, pages are constantly being written to disk and then being read back and the operating system is too busy to allow much real work to be performed.

Linux uses a Least Recently Used (LRU) page aging technique to fairly choose pages, which might be removed from the system. This scheme involves every page in the system having an age, which changes as the page is accessed. The more that a page is accessed, the younger it is; the less that it is accessed the older and more stale it becomes. Old pages are good candidates for swapping.

Linux File Systems

One of the most important features of Linux is its support for many different file systems. This makes it very flexible and well able to coexist with many other operating systems. Linux supports several file systems including minix, ext, ext2, ext3, ext4,Reiserfs, XFS, JFS, xia, msdos, umsdos, vfat, ntfs, proc, nfs, iso9660, hpfs, sysv, smb, ncpfs

Ext2 is Linux's default file system and is widely used. The Linux file systems are implemented using a VFS(Virtual File system) layer.

Virtual File Systems

Linux uses a virtual, unified file system model. This means that the file systems that reside on different disks and in different partitions are not accessed by a unique drive letter (like Windows does), but are all *mounted* on top of each other in a huge, virtual file system. This offers transparency to users, makes system administration easier, and makes it possible to support far more than 26 different file systems simultaneously. The first file system is called the *root file system* and is mounted by the kernel itself, when the kernel starts. In addition to regular directories and data, this file system also contains a number of empty directories, which are used as mount points for other file systems. As an example, take a look at /dev/hda6 in the figure below. It is a fully contained file system, with its own directories and files. One of the directories is called *log*. When this file system is mounted on the *var* directory in the root file system, the *log* directory now becomes available in our virtual file system hierarchy as /*var*/*log*. But you also could have mounted /dev/hda6 on, let's say, the mount point (empty directory) *variable* in the root file system (/dev/hda2). Then all of a sudden, the *log* directory would have become available as /*variable*/*log*.

- Linux does not use drive letters (A:, C:, D:) to identify drives/partitions, but creates a virtual, unified filesystem.
- Different drivers/partitions are *mounted* on a *mountpoint*.

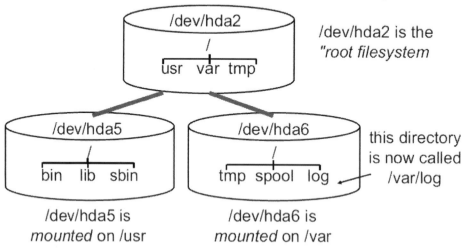

Sketch 2.6 Drive mounts in a Linux file system

Interprocess Communication in Linux

Processes communicate with each other and with the Linux kernel to co-ordinate their activities. Linux supports a number of IPC mechanisms, signals and pipes being most significant ones. Linux also supports sockets and System V IPC mechanism.

IPC - Signals

If you want to control a process from outside the shell (or other process) that started it, you need to use signals. Signals are the UNIX way of "nudging" a process into doing something. When a process is running in the foreground, you can use keyboard interrupts (Ctrl-*key*) to send a signal. Otherwise, you need to use the kill or killall command to send a signal. Most signals are delivered to the application itself. Technically, this means that the programmer of an application can write a special subroutine (called a signal handler) that is executed when a signal arrives. If the programmer did not write these special signal handlers, then the kernel performs the default action for that signal, which in most cases means that the application is terminated. For us, only a few signals are important.

- 0-31 standard signals and 32-64 real-time configurable
- Used to send asynchronous events to one or more processes
- Signals are like software interrupt and unidirectional
- Signals are used to exit processes, kill programs etc.
- Signals are delivered in system mode and received in user mode
- Received signals can be Accepted, Ignored, Blocked, or Handled (at later time)

Linux Pipes

In Linux, a pipe is implemented using two file data structures which both point at the same temporary VFS inode which itself points at a physical page within memory. Each file data structure contains pointers to different file operation routine vectors; one for writing to the pipe, the other for reading from the pipe.

This hides the underlying differences from the generic system calls, which read and write to ordinary files. As the writing process writes to the pipe, bytes are copied into the shared data page and when the reading process reads from the pipe, bytes are copied from the shared data page. Linux must synchronize access to the pipe. It must make sure that the reader and the writer of the pipe are in step and to do this it uses locks, wait queues and signals.

When the writer wants to write to the pipe it uses the standard write library functions. These all pass file descriptors that are indices into the process's set of file data structures, each one representing an open file or, as in this case, an open pipe. The Linux system call uses the write routine pointed at by the file data structure describing this pipe. That write routine uses information held in the VFS inode representing the pipe to manage the write request.

If there is enough room to write all of the bytes into the pipe and, so long as the pipe is not locked by its reader, Linux locks it for the writer and copies the bytes to be written from the processes address space into the shared data page. If the pipe is locked by the reader or if there is not enough room for the data then the current process is made to sleep on the pipe inode's wait queue and the scheduler is called so that another process can run. It is interruptible, so it can receive signals and it will be woken by the reader when there is enough room for the write data or when the pipe is unlocked. When the data has been written, the pipe's VFS inode is unlocked and any waiting readers sleeping on the inode's wait queue will themselves be woken up. Reading data from the pipe is a very similar process to writing to it.

Processes are allowed to do non-blocking reads (it depends on the mode in which they opened the file or pipe) and, in this case, if there is no data to be read or if the pipe is locked, an error will be returned. This means that the process can continue to run. The alternative is to wait on the pipe inode's wait queue until the write process has finished. When both processes have finished with the pipe, the pipe inode is discarded along with the shared data page.

Linux also supports *named* pipes, also known as FIFOs because pipes operate on a First In, First Out principle. The first data written into the pipe is the first data read from the pipe. Unlike pipes, FIFOs are not temporary objects; they are entities in the file system and can be created using the mkfifo command. Processes are free to use a FIFO so long as they have appropriate access rights to it. The way that FIFOs are opened is a little different from pipes. A pipe (its two file data structures, its VFS inode and the shared data page) is created in one go whereas a FIFO already exists and is opened and closed by its users. Linux must handle readers opening the FIFO before writers open it as well as readers reading before any writers have written to it. That aside, FIFOs are handled almost exactly the same way as pipes and they use the same data structures and operations.

SystemV IPC

Linux supports three types of interprocess communication mechanisms; these are message queues, semaphores and shared memory. These System V IPC mechanisms all share common authentication methods. Processes may access these resources only by passing a unique reference identifier to the kernel via system calls.

Message Queues

Message queues can be considered as an internal linked list within kernel's address space. Message queues allow one or more processes to write messages, which will be read by one or more reading processes. Linux kernel maintains a linked list of messages, labeled by unique identifiers. When message queues are created a new data structure is allocated from system memory and inserted into the vector. Messages are added to the end of the queue. Messages can be removed from front, middle or anywhere like voice mail.

Semaphores

Linux uses semaphores to allow just one process at a time to access critical regions of code and data; all other processes wishing to access this resource will be made to wait until it becomes free. A Linux semaphore data structure contains the following information:

Count - keeps track of the count of processes wishing to use this resource. A positive value means that the resource is available. A negative or zero value means that processes are waiting for it. An initial value of 1 means one and only one process at a time can use this resource. When processes want this resource they decrement the count and when they have finished with this resource they increment the count.

Waking - is the count of processes waiting for this resource, which is also the number of process waiting to be awakened when this resource becomes free.

wait queue - when processes are waiting for this resource they are put onto this wait queue.

Lock - a buzz lock used when accessing the waking field.

Suppose the initial count for a semaphore is 1, the first process to come along will see that the count is positive and decrement it by 1, making it 0. The process now ``owns" the critical piece of code or resource that is being protected by the semaphore. When a process leaves the critical region, it increments the semaphore's count. The most optimal case is where there are no other processes contending for ownership of the critical region. Linux has implemented semaphores to work efficiently for this, the most common case.

If another process wishes to enter the critical region whilst it is owned by a process it too will decrement the count. As the count is now negative (-1) the process cannot enter the critical region. Instead it must wait until the owning process exits it. Linux makes the waiting process sleep until the owning process wakes it on exiting the critical region. The waiting process adds itself to the semaphore's wait queue and sits in a loop checking the value of the waking field and calling the scheduler until waking is non-zero.

Shared Memory

Shared memory allows one or more processes to communicate via memory that appears in all of their virtual address spaces. It is the fastest IPC mechanism since there is no intermediation between processes. Information is directly mapped from a memory segment to address space of a calling process once the memory is being shared, there are no checks on how the processes are using it. They must rely on other mechanisms, for example System V semaphores, to synchronize access to the memory.

Linux Containers (LXC)

Linux containers allow OS level virtualization on a single Linux instance. Unlike virtualization using Hypervisor technique, Linux containers do not need separate kernel instances to run on giving flexibility to create large amount of containers with faster startup and shutdown speeds. Containers are based on shared operating systems, they are much leaner and faster than hypervisors.

LXC aims to provide creation of a Linux environment as close as possible as a standard Linux install without the need for a separate kernel. LXC relies on two different feature sets of the Linux kernel: kernel namespaces and control groups. Kernel namespaces provide basic isolation making sure that each container cannot see or affect other containers. Control groups on the other hand are used to allocate resources such as memory, CPU and I/O between containers.

Why should you use Linux containers (LXC)?

1. Containers are still virtualization.
    a. Each container has its own network interface (and IP addresses)
    b. Each container has its own file system
    c. Each container is well isolated for security and resource usage
2. Containers are small footprint
    a. On a typical physical machine with average computing resources, you can easily run 100-1000 containers compared to 10-100 virtual machines.
    b. On disk, containers can be very light
3. Containers are fast
    a. They deployed fast and boots fast in seconds

What are the use cases of Linux containers (LXC)?

- Developers use it for continuous integration; test team can run faster tests after each commit, run multiple tests in isolation in multiple containers. They also solve the dependency problem as build and run in a controlled environment.
- Managed service providers use container for cheaper hosting. They can provide free and trial services much more easily and in-expensively using containers. Resources can be brought up and down to save money.

LXC lifecycle is defined by the following steps and associated commands:

- Setup a container (root file system and config) using lxc-create
- Boot the container (by default, you get a console) lxc-start
- Attach a console (if you started in background) lxc-console
- Shutdown the container lxc-stop
- Destroy the file system created with lxc-create lxc-destroy

A Linux container can be setup in the Ubuntu distribution by following simple steps here: https://help.ubuntu.com/12.04/serverguide/lxc.html

Namespaces

Linux namespaces partition essential kernel structures to create virtual environments. For example, you can have multiple processes with pid 67, in different environments. Linux currently implements 6 different types of namespaces as described below. The purpose of these namespaces is to abstract a particular set of global system resources in a such a way that to a process within the same namespace, it appears to have a its own isolated instance of the global resource. One of the goal of the namespaces was to support the implementation of containers. However in order to use Linux containers, you don't have to use all namespaces.

Mount namespaces: isolate the file system mount points visible to a group of processes. Therefore processes in different mount namespaces can have different views of the file systems One use of mount namespaces is to create environments using chroot( ) system call. However, by contrast with the use of the chroot() system call, mount namespaces are a more secure and flexible tool for this task. Other sophisticated uses of mount namespaces are also possible. For example, separate mount namespaces can be set up in a master-slave relationship, so that the mount events are automatically propagated from one namespace to another. Mount namespaces were first type of namespace implemented in Linux in 2002.

UTS namespaces: isolate two system identifiers nodename and domainname returned by the uname() system call; the names are set using the sethostname() and setdomainname() system calls. In the context of containers, the UTS namespaces feature allow each container to have its own hostname and NIS domain name. This can be useful for initialization and configuration scripts that tailor their actions based on these names. The term "UTS" derives from the name of the structure passed to the uname() system call: struct utsname. The name of that structure in turn derives from "UNIX Time-sharing System".

IPC namespaces: isolate certain interprocess communication (IPC) resources, namely, system v ipc objects and (since Linux 2.6.3 POSIX message queues. The common characteristic of these IPC mechanisms is that IPC objects are identified by mechanisms other than filesystem pathnames. Each IPC namespace has its own set of System V IPC identifiers and its own POSIX message queue filesystem.

PID namespaces: isolate the process ID number space. In other words, processes in different PID namespaces can have the same PID. One of the main benefits of PID namespaces is that containers can be migrated between hosts while keeping the same process IDs for the processes inside the container. PID namespaces also allow each container to have its own init (PID 1), the "ancestor of all processes" that manages various system initialization tasks and reaps orphaned child processes when they terminate.

Net namespaces: provide isolation of the system resources associated with networking. Thus, each network namespace has its own network devices, IP addresses, IP routing tables, /proc/net directory, port numbers, and so on. Network namespaces make containers useful from a networking perspective: each container can have its own (virtual) network device and its own applications for example, it is possible to have multiple containerized web servers on the same host system, with each server bound to port 80 in its (per-container) network namespace.

User namespaces: isolate the user and group ID number spaces. In other words, a process's user and group IDs can be different inside and outside a user namespace. The most interesting case here is that a process can have a normal unprivileged user ID outside a user namespace while at the same time having a user ID of 0 inside the namespace. This means that the process has full root privileges for operations inside the user namespace, but is unprivileged for operations outside the namespace.

Control groups

Linux control groups (cgroups) allow you to limit, account, and isolate resource usage by putting processes within control groups. You can think of cgroups as ulimit but for groups of processes with fine-grained accounting. Control groups are exposed as virtual file systems. Here is how you utilize control groups.

create a cgroup: *mkdir /cgroup/helloworld*

move process pid 5679 to the cgroup: *echo 5679 > /cgroup/helloworld/tasks* limit memory usage: *echo 512000 > /cgroup/helloworld/memory.limit_in_bytes*

Docker

Applications like Docker (https://www.docker.com/tryit/) are built on top of LXC. (requires Linux 3.8+ kernel) Docker is a toolset with several powerful functionalities, which makes packaging of application a breeze for cloud deployment. According to the creator of the tool, *Docker is an open-source engine that automates the deployment of any application as a lightweight, portable, self-sufficient container that will run virtually anywhere.*

Docker defines a format for packaging an application and all its dependencies into a single container, which can be transferred to any docker-enabled machine, and executed there with the guarantee that the execution environment exposed to the application, will be the same. Lxc implements process sandboxing, which is an important pre-requisite for portable deployment, but that alone is not enough for portable deployment. Docker abstracts hardware-specific settings, so that the exact same docker container can run unchanged on many different machines, with many different configurations.

Docker includes a tool for developers to automatically assemble a container from their source code, with full control over application dependencies, build tools, packaging etc. They are free to use tools like make, maven, chef, puppet, salt, debian packages, rpms, source tarballs, or any combination of the above, regardless of the configuration of the machines. Docker includes git-like capabilities for tracking versions of a container, inspecting the diff between versions, committing new versions, rolling back etc. The history also includes how a container was assembled and by whom, so you get full traceability from the production server all the way back to the upstream developer. Docker also implements incremental uploads and downloads, similar to "git pull", so new versions of a container can be transferred by only sending diffs. Any container can be used as an "base image" to create more specialized components. This can be done manually or as part of an automated build. Docker has access to a public registry (https://registry.hub.docker.com/) where thousands of users have uploaded useful containers. The registry also includes an official "standard library" of useful containers maintained by the docker team. The registry itself is open-source, so anyone can deploy their own registry to store and transfer private containers, for internal server deployments.

Why are docker containers lightweight?

Unlike VMs where every app, every copy of an app and even slight modification of the app requires a new VM, in a container:

- You don't need OS that takes up resource, space and does not require startup.
- When you make a copy of the app, still no OS. App can share bins and libs.
- When you modify the app, Copy on Write feature allows to only save the diffs between original container and modified container.

Exercise:

1. What command would you use to copy the file /home/tux1/mydoc to /tmp, and rename it at the same time to tempdoc?
2. If a process is hanging, what is the proper order of terminating it with the lowest chance of data corruption?
3. What is a daemon?
4. Translate the following command into your native language:
5. **ls -lR | egrep"txt$|tab$"| sort -rn+4 | tail +4 | head -5**
6. Write a one-line script that will multiply any two numbers together.
7. Does Linux operating system provide an undelete utility to recover deleted files? Justify your answer with why / why not. Is there any way to recover accidently deleted files on Linux?
8. In Linux operating system boot process
9. What is the first process to execute when the Linux kernel is loaded?
10. What could happen, if kernel cannot execute this process?

Project:

1. Learn docker basics by completing the tutorial at docker website: https://www.docker.com/tryit/
2. Dockerize a simple web application (written by you) and publish to the repository for others to use. Follow these instructions:
   a. Docker daemon only runs on Linux, you will need Boot2docker – a lightweight Linux distribution based on tiny coreLinux made specifically to run docker http://boot2docker.io/

Databases & Information Management

Chapter Goal

After studying this chapter, you should be able to:

- Refresh your database system concepts and learn about some of emerging database systems
- Refresh data modeling knowledge and concepts and learn to apply them in data ware house and business intelligence arena

Introduction to Databases

"When people use the word database, fundamentally what they are saying is that the data should be self-describing and it should have a schema. That's really all the word database means." - Jim Gray, "The Fourth Paradigm"

Modern databases solve mainly these four problems:

- Sharing – Multiple readers and writers can share data concurrently. This became extremely important when business transactions needed to be facilitated into the database and till date, online transaction processing or OLTP is the major purpose companies invest in databases.
- Enforcement of Data Model – Databases are used in business enterprise to support hundreds if not thousands of applications such as finance, payroll, recruitment, retention, shipping, vendor acquisition etc. All

applications must be able to use clean organize data that are compliant to the data model used by the organization. This is also referred as Relational Database constraints or Referential Integrity.

- Scalability – Modern relation databases allow both scale up and scale out. Scaling up topology allows large data sets to fit in server's main memory. It also utilizes Multi-core parallelism to parallelize query execution for faster results. Scale out topology allows adding multiple servers to distribute data and query execution. This can be shared nothing architecture where no memory, CPU or disks are shared between the systems or shared memory system where CPU and disks are not shared.

- Flexibility – modern databases support hybrid storage layer such as IBM DB2 supports native XML storage side by side its relational storage and the new columnar storage. These built-in features enable wide variety of industry standards and variety of applications to use databases in different ways.

What is a Data Warehouse?

A data warehouse is used to support forecasting and decision-making processes across the enterprise. It acts as a centralized repository of an organization's data, ultimately providing a comprehensive and homogenized view of the organization.

Traditional database systems are designed to support typical day-to-day operations via individual user transactions (e.g. registering for a course, entering a financial transaction, etc.). Such systems are generally called operational or transactional systems.

A data warehouse complements an existing operational system and is therefore designed and subsequently used quite differently. While an operational system is transaction or process-oriented, a data warehouse is subject-oriented, geared toward flexible analytical processing of high volumes of business data. Typical data warehouse architecture below shows necessary components

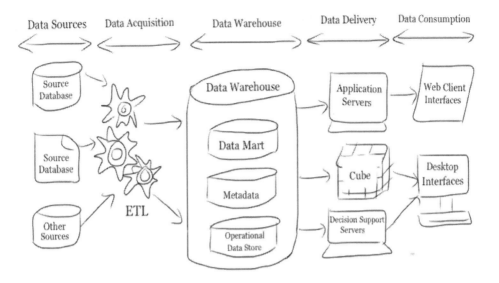

Sketch 3.1 Data warehouse component architecture

What are emerging technologies in Database arena?

Columnar Database Technology

Columnar Database Technology stores content by columns rather than row. The 2-D data represented at conceptual level will be mapped to 1-D data structure at physical level. Comparing with Row based storage where all the information about one entity is stored together, in columnar storage all attribute information are stored together.

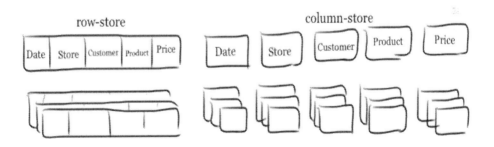

Sketch 3.2 Row vs. Column data store

In the context of data analytics, data input/output I/O has become the true bottleneck in data processing today. Database researchers have been developing ways to get only data in memory that is needed. If you get more data than it is required for specific query processing then you cannot achieve the real time performance that is expected today. Columnar databases provide the way to pick the columns needed instead of retrieving the entire row where you end up not using all the columns that are part of that row. This is a huge reduction in overhead as most of analytic queries make use of one or two columns only. Columnar storage technology offers a better solution in the use cases where the query workload needs a small percentage of the overall column bytes.

In-Memory Database Technology

Database researchers have long recognized that grabbing data from main memory is much faster than grabbing it from the disk. They have been partially achieving this idea by implementing caching in databases, in which database engine predicts which data will be requested next and keep that in main memory. However, with the growing demand for real time database systems, caching does not seem to solve the problem of latency. Especially in other than read, in write and update it has to finally save data to disk via cache. In memory databases implement way to read and manipulate data in main memory. By keeping all records in main memory at all times, In-memory databases eliminate obvious sources of latency, such as physical disk I/O and cache management, as well as less obvious ones, such as reliance on the underlying file system to store and organize data. The result is sorting, storage and retrieval of records dramatically faster than is possible with traditional DBMSs.

In-memory databases are used in diverse domain such as financial trading, mobile ad network, telecom network equipment and wireless gears. Some prominent vendors in this space are SolidDB and Sybase ASE. An in-memory database system can provide virtually all of the features of a traditional DBMS. These include a high-level data definition language (DDL); programming interfaces, such as ODBC, JDBC or native C/C++ or Java APIs; transactions that support the ACID (Atomic, Consistent, Isolated and Durable) properties; features for database durability, such as transaction logging; database indexes, event notifications, multi-user concurrency, and more.

Temporal Database Technology

In database world, there are two types of times that are important, system time and business time. System time involves tracking when changes are made to the state of a table such as when a particular transaction was made or insurance policy was changed. Business time sometimes also referred as application time involves tracking the effective dates of certain business conditions, such as terms of an insurance policy or change in interest rate of a loan. Some businesses need to track both business time and system time in a table; such tables are called bi-temporal table.

Web Database Technology

Web databases allow you to create and manage database online. These databases are lightweight and provide good support for SaaS based application. Most web database comes with integrated application development platform. Some examples of web database are:

- Intuit Quickbase
- database.com
- Google AppEngine Data Model
- Baseportal
- Zoho

Database Index Overview

You can think of an index as a table of contents for tables. If it's there, the database knows where to look more specific. If it isn't there, the database has to search through all the data to find it. By creating an index on one or more columns of a table, you gain the ability in some cases to retrieve a small set of randomly distributed rows from the table. Indexes are one of many means of reducing disk I/O.

If a table has no indexes, then the database must perform a full table scan to find a value. For example, without an index, a query of suppliers in a Supplier table requires the database to search every row in every table block for this value. This approach does not scale well as data volumes increase.

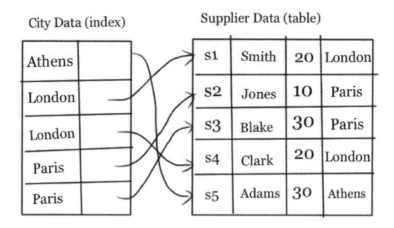

Sketch 3.3 A city data index on Supplier table

An index on City makes a DBMS efficient to find all suppliers in that city. Like tables, indexes consist of rows and columns but store the data in a logically sorted manner to improve search performance. This sorting makes it possible to find all entries for a specific order (Alphabetically or range) quickly.

You can have many indexes on the same table but on different columns. So, an index on lastname, firstname is different from an index on firstname only (which you would need to optimize searches by first name). Indexes hold redundant data. They have the same information as stored in the table, but in a sorted manner. This redundancy is automatically maintained by the database for each write operation you perform (insert/update/delete). Consequently, indexes decrease write performance. Besides finding data quickly, indexes can also be used to optimize sort operations (order by) and physically arrange related data closely together (data clustering).

Indexes are used in two different ways:
- Sequential access - sequence of values in the index file. This also works for range queries (e.g. find suppliers whose city is in alphabetical range)
- Direct access - direct access to the index value supplied as query parameter. This is also used for list queries (e.g. find suppliers whose city is in the specified list).

Query Optimization in Databases

In order to understand query optimization in databases, we need to understand why it is necessary. Let's take an example query: "Get all vendor names who supply case for iPhone 5"

Select distinct vendor.vendorname from vendor, Case where vendor.vendor# = Case.vendor# and Case.PhoneType = 'iPhone 5'

If the database contains 100 vendors and 10,000 types of phone cases, of which only 50 are iPhone 5 cases and database engine has to execute this query without doing any optimization, then the sequence of the execution will be something like the following:

1. Calculate the Cartesian product of the two tables Vendor and Case. This step will read 10100 tuples and produce 100 * 10000 = 1,000,000 tuples
2. Take the results of step 1 through WHERE clause which again involves reading 1,000,000 tuples and producing about 50 tuples
3. Projection of the result achieved in step 2 over VendorName to produce the desired final count

Now let's look at the following sequence of execution which is similar to the previous one but obviously much more efficient than the first one:

1. Read only tuples of Case table for PhoneType 'iPhone 5'. This will involve reading 10,000 tuples but produces only 50 tuples and keep in main memory
2. Join the results of step1 to the table Vendor over Vendor#(requires retrieval of only 100 tuples) and produces 50 tuples (still in main memory)
3. Projection of the result from step2 over vendorName to produce final result.

We know that I/O due to reading tuples from the disk is the main bottleneck in the database engine performance. Hence any way, we can reduce this I/O will significantly enhance the query performance. This example is enough to explain why query optimization is necessary. SQL and XQuery compiler performs several steps to produce an access plan that can be executed.

- While compiling the statements the query optimizer estimates the execution cost of different ways of satisfying the query.
- Optimizer uses sorting when no index satisfies requested ordering of data or thinks it's less expensive than index scan.
- Optimizer uses Group and sort pushdown when necessary:

select workdept, avg(salary) as avg_dept_salary from employee group by workdept

Business Modeling

Business modeling is a formal representation of business information: its objects, the object's properties or attributes, and the relationships of one object to another. It serves as a verification of the users' view of the business before the database is even designed. Business models can be created as Entity Relationship Diagram (ERD), which provides a pictorial representation of the user's view of the business.

Business modeling is not based on how the data is going to be stored or on which platform the applications will run. It is focused on business, not technology. It is not dependent upon the underlying database structure or a specific application. The business model has many parts and there is no formal definition of what parts must exist to be a valid model.

An example of a business model would be naming the major business entities (objects) of a company such as department, employee, projects and their relationship with each other.

An entity relationship diagram can go further and convert business entities into data entities where many-to-many relationships are resolved, primary and foreign keys are identified, and repeating data elements are discovered and result in additional data entities.

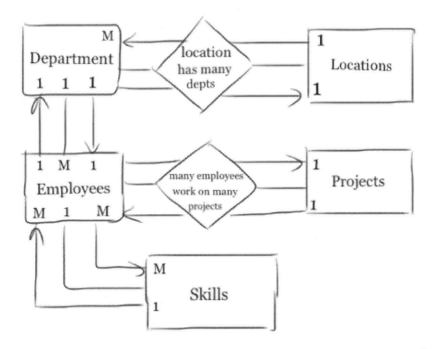

Sketch 3.4 Database ER diagram

Database Design with Normalization

Normalization is the process of steps that will identify, for elimination, redundancies in a database design. Data normalization is part of the database design process. Once the entities, their relationships, the primary keys, and foreign keys are identified, the next step is to define all the non-key elements or properties for a given entity. Once the columns are defined, it is time to consider normalizing your tables. There are five different levels of normalization and the first three are almost always done – that is why we won't go into detail about the last 2. Always normalize to the Third Normal Form first and then go back and do any denormalizing based on user needs – this is good practice. Normalization solves many problems and keeps your data model flexible. A drawback is that it may impact performance based on user requirements.

1NF: eliminate repeating groups

Relational tables must have the same number of rows and columns and each column must mean the same thing in the same sequence in each row. Let's take a look at the table below:

EMP NO	LAST NAME	WORK DEPT	DEPT NAME	SKILL 1	SKILL2	SKILLN...
000030	KWAN	GRE	OPERATIONS	141		
000250	SMITH	BLU	PLANNING	002	011	067
000270	PEREZ	RED	MARKETING	415	447	
000300	SMITH	BLU	PLANNING	011	032	

In the employee table, if you wanted to show that each employee had multiple skills, you would need to create an additional table where each skill for a given employee is represented in a row. The unique identifier here would be the employee number and the skill number. If a new skill is created and an employee already has the maximum number of skills allocated in the data structure, then the entire file structure and all the programs have to be changed. If this table is normalized, then the new skill simply becomes a new row.

EMP NO	LAST NAME	WORK DEPT	DEPT NAME
000030	KWAN	GRE	OPERATIONS
000250	SMITH	BLU	PLANNING
000270	PEREZ	RED	MARKETING
00030	SMITH	BLU	PLANNING

EMP NO	SKILL	SKILL DESC
000030	141	RESEARCH
000250	002	BID PREP
000250	011	NEGOTIATION
000250	067	PROD SPEC
000270	415	BENEFITS ANL
000270	447	TESTING
000300	011	NEGOTIATION
000300	032	INV CONTROL

Suppose you kept the monthly salary within the employee table. So you would have a maximum number of 12 separate salaries for a given person. This would violate the rule of a fixed number of columns for each row and you would not be able to use the column functions of the SQL language against this information.

2NF: eliminate columns that depend only on part of the key

What are the three problems with the 1NF EMP_SKILLTABLE?

Here, the skills of the company have been matched with the employees in a separate table where the skill description is also included. The skill description depends only upon the skill number. Here are 3 problems that arise:
1. The skill description will be repeated every time the skill is repeated.

2. If this description for the skill changes, then multiple rows will need to be changed, risking some "update anomalies" (data inconsistencies are due to not changing all the rows).
3. If an employee is the sole source for a given skill and that person leaves the company, that particular skill and skill description is lost forever ("delete anomaly").

How do you solve these problems? By creating another table that holds the skill number and skill description.

EMP_SKILL TABLE   SKILL DESC TABLE

EMP NO	SKILL	DATE CERT	SKILL	SKILL DESC
000030	141		141	RESEARCH
000250	002		002	BID PREP
000250	011		011	NEGOTIATION
000250	067		067	PROD SPEC
000270	415		415	BENEFITS ANL
000270	447		447	TESTING
000300	011		011	NEGOTIATION
000300	032		032	INV CONTROL

Let's look at the Employee table again.

EMP NO	LAST NAME	WORK DEPT	DEPT NAME	MGRNO	...
000030	KWAN	GRE	OPERATIONS	000080	
000250	SMITH	BLU	PLANNING	000010	
000270	PEREZ	RED	MARKETING	000020	
000300	SMITH	BLU	PLANNING	000010	

Here, the department number is located in the employee table which shows the relationship between the employee and department tables – many employees work for one department and that the Department Name columns is a fact about the Department Number column. The employee number is the primary key. The same three problems arise just like the problems in the second normal form and they can be solved the same way. Add an additional table where the Department Number is the primary key and the Department Name is dependent on it.

EMP NO	LASTNAME	WORK DEPT	...	WORK DEPT	DEPT NAME	MGRNO
000030	KWAN	GRE		GRE	OPERATIONS	000080
000250	SMITH	BLU		BLU	PLANNING	000010
000270	PEREZ	RED		RED	MARKETING	000020
00030	SMITH	BLU		BLU	PLANNING	000010

Cost & Benefits of Normalization

Let's look at the cost and benefits of Normalization by using the two tables EMPL and DEPT.

Case #1 Normalized to 2 Tables

EMPL   (EMPNO, DEPT, LAST, MI, FIRST, JOB)
1,000,000 rows   30 chars / row

DEPT   (DEPT, DEPTNAME, MGRNO)
10,000 rows   25 chars / row

Employee One with a million 30-character rows and a related table with 10,000 25-character rows. Let's consider that a critical transaction runs 20,000 times a day and requires data from these two tables in each transaction.

Transaction rate 20,000 per day, two tables accessed.

SELECT LAST, MI, FIRST, MGRNO   FROM EMPL A, DEPT B

WHERE A.DEPT = B.DEPT AND   EMPNO = '000010'

Case #2 De-normalization

Denormalization could improve the performance of our critical transaction. An alternative is to carry MGRNO in both tables; in DEPT, where it can be used by other applications; and in EMPL, where it can improve the performance of our critical transaction. The objective is to produce the critical report and avoid the performance cost of a join.

```
┌─────────────────┐     (EMPNO, DEPT, LAST, MI, FIRST, MGRNO)
│      EMPL       │         1,000,000 rows
└─────────────────┘            30 chars / row
```

```
┌─────────────────┐     (DEPT, DEPTNAME, MGRNO)
│      DEPT       │         10,000 rows
└─────────────────┘            25 chars / row
```

Storage Cost

1,000,000 rows x 3 characters = 3,000,000 characters (Approx. 900 pages)

Additional updates if MGRNO changes

Save 20000 accesses per day

Data Modeling

In Data Modeling, each business entity will become a data entity. A data entity is something about which we store data. Once the business entities and their relationships to each other have been defined, it is time to proceed to the data modeling steps. The data modeling steps consists of turning the business entities and then determining the attributes or properties of each of the entities. The attributes will eventually become the columns in the database tables.

Tables and Columns

A general starting point is one table per entity. The remaining processes will help to identify entities that we didn't realize we had also to identify additional tables that must be created to support our data in a relational database. Each data element will become a column in our tables. Each attribute of an entity will be a column in the entity's table. There is a need for proper column granularity. Example: If a search will be by street name, then you should consider storing the numbers portion of the street address separately from the street name portion. City, state, country code, or zip code should be stored in their own columns, too.

NULL Characteristics

A null characteristic is a data processing rule that we want database to follow when the value for a particular column for a given row is unknown. There are 3 null characteristics:

NOT NULL: Column must always have a value

NOT NULL WITH DEFAULT: Column must always have a value – if we don't supply one, Database does

NULLABLE: Column can be marked as having an 'unknown value'

Data Relationships

Data relationships are designed into our tables A row in one table may be associated with a row or rows in another table. A row in one table can carry a value from some table's unique key, for example. each employee row contains the value of the employee's department KEY

Primary Key

The PRIMARY KEY constraint uniquely identifies each record in a database table. Primary keys must contain unique values. A primary key column cannot contain NULL values. Consider you have a STUDENTS table that contains a record for each student at a university. The student's unique student ID number would be a good choice for a primary key in the STUDENTS table. The student's first and last name would not be a good choice, as there is always the chance that more than one student might have the same name. So, a primary key best identifies the data being stored in the table.

Unique Key

Unique key is a column or set of columns that contain unique values. Without a unique key, you may not be able to find a specific row in the table. One of the unique keys can be defined to DBMS as being the primary key of the table.

Foreign Key

A foreign key is a column or set of columns that contains values from some table's unique key. A foreign key is created into tables to define relationships between rows.

Referential Integrity

Referential integrity ensures that the relationship between two tables' remains synchronized during updates and deletes. A DBMS follows rules to enforce Referential Integrity such as:

- A foreign key value must match a unique key value or be null
- Primary key values cannot be null
- All non-null values must match a value in the referenced column (column set)

Referential Integrity- Delete rules - ON DELATE CASCADE

The referenced table is the department table. The foreign key EMPL.DEP was defined with an ON DELATE CASCADE rule.

DEP	DEPNAME	MANAGER	DIVISION
BLU	PLANNING	000020	EASTERN
GRE	OPERATIONS	000080	WESTERN
RED	MARKETING	000010	EASTERN

EMPNO	LASTNAME	FIRSTNAME	DEP	GOVT_ID	SALARY
000010	HAAS	CHRISTINE	RED	888-88-2794	52750.00
000020	THOMPSON	MICHAEL	BLU	888-89-4261	31000.00
000030	KWAN	SALLY	GRE	888-88-9456	33000.00

If you delete the BLU DEP row from the department table with ON DELETE CASCADE as the delete rule, all employees in the BLU DEP are also deleted.

DEP	DEPNAME	MANAGER	DIVISION
GRE	OPERATIONS	000080	WESTERN
RED	MARKETING	000010	EASTERN

EMPNO	LASTNAME	FIRSTNAME	DEP	GOVT_ID	SALARY
000010	HAAS	CHRISTINE	RED	888-88-2794	52750.00
000030	KWAN	SALLY	GRE	888-88-9456	33000.00

Referential Integrity- Delete rules - ON DELATE SET NULL

The referenced table is the department table. The foreign key EMPL.DEP was defined with an ON DELETE SET NULL rule.

DEP	DEPNAME	MANAGER	DIVISION
BLU	PLANNING	000020	EASTERN
GRE	OPERATIONS	000080	WESTERN
RED	MARKETING	000010	EASTERN

EMPNO	LASTNAME	FIRSTNAME	DEP	GOVT_ID	SALARY
000010	HAAS	CHRISTINE	RED	888-88-2794	52750.00
000020	THOMPSON	MICHAEL	BLU	888-89-4261	31000.00
000030	KWAN	SALLY	GRE	888-88-9456	33000.00

When the BLU DEP row is deleted from the department table, RDBMS will set up the DEP value for all BLUE DEP employees to null.

DEP	DEPNAME	MANAGER	DIVISION
GRE	OPERATIONS	000080	WESTERN
RED	MARKETING	000010	EASTERN

EMPNO	LASTNAME	FIRSTNAME	DEP	GOVT_ID	SALARY
000010	HAAS	CHRISTINE	RED	888-88-2794	52750.00
000020	THOMPSON	MICHAEL		888-89-4261	31000.00
000030	KWAN	SALLY	GRE	888-88-9456	33000.00

Referential Integrity- Delete rules - ON DELATE RESTRICT

The referenced table is the department table. The foreign key EMPL.DEP was defined with an ON DELETE RESTRICT rule. Before RDBMS will allow the BLU DEP row to be deleted from the department table, it checks to ensure that there are no employee rows with BLU DEP values.

DEP	DEPNAME	MANAGER	DIVISION
BLU	PLANNING	000020	EASTERN
GRE	OPERATIONS	000080	WESTERN
RED	MARKETING	000010	EASTERN

EMPNO	LASTNAME	FIRSTNAME	DEP	GOVT_ID	SALARY
000010	HAAS	CHRISTINE	RED	888-88-2794	52750.00
000020	THOMPSON	MICHAEL	BLU	888-89-4261	31000.00
000030	KWAN	SALLY	GRE	888-88-9456	33000.00

If RDBMS finds one employee row with a value of BLU in the DEP column, the delete fails (is restricted).

DEP	DEPNAME	MANAGER	DIVISION
BLU	PLANNING	000020	EASTERN
GRE	OPERATIONS	000080	WESTERN
RED	MARKETING	000010	EASTERN

EMPNO	LASTNAME	FIRSTNAME	DEP	SOC_SEC	SALARY
000010	HAAS	CHRISTINE	RED	888-88-2794	52750.00
000020	THOMPSON	MICHAEL		888-89-4261	31000.00
000030	KWAN	SALLY	GRE	888-88-9456	33000.00

A Business Intelligence System

The following is the abstract from the paper published in 2nd issue of IBM journal of Research & Development in Oct 1958:

"An automatic system is being developed to disseminate information to the various sections of any industrial, scientific or government organization. This intelligence system will utilize data-processing machines for auto-abstracting and auto-encoding of documents and for creating interest profiles for each of the "action points" in an organization. Both incoming and internally generated documents are automatically abstracted, characterized by a word pattern, and sent automatically to appropriate action points. This paper shows the flexibility of such a system in identifying known information, in finding that needs to know it and in disseminating it efficiently either in abstract form or as a complete document."

From Luhn's vision to the current state of BI

- 1970 - E. F. Codd an IBM researcher first proposed the relational model for data
- Mid-1970 - IBM had a working prototype of a relational database management system (RDBMS)
- 1980 - RDBMS's use was proliferating.
- 1983 – Teradata sold the first relational database designed specifically for decision support to Wells Fargo.
- 1986 - Ralph Kimball founded Red Brick Systems (part of IBM now) to build databases for the same market.
- 1991 - Bill Inmon's *Building the Data Warehouse* (Wiley) was published. Inmon advocated creating Enterprise data model.
- 1995 – Inmon's book was a big hit. TDWI was formed.

- 1996 – Ralph Kimball published The Data warehouse Toolkit, challenged the EDM and advocated the data mart model
- 1997 – Microsoft researchers introduced cube (multi-dimensional data model)
- 2000 – BI Platforms emerging
- 2005 – BI appliances maximizing ROI
- 2009 – Smarter Analytics platform emerging
- 2012 – Big Data Analytics and Business Intelligence are merging

Why do companies need a Business Intelligence (BI) Platform?

Every business needs at least a simple BI platform for:

- Discovering deeper business insights from the tons of data they have. Unlocking the potential of data in a company is CIO's #1 priority right now. They need to uncover trends and anomalies in the data to maximize profitability, minimize customer churn, detect fraud and increase campaign effectiveness.
- Getting fast answers to business questions. Business need to deliver right information to decision makers where, when and how they need it.
- Making better faster decisions. Business need to align decisions across the organization with interactive, self-service environments for exploration and analysis
- Optimizing Business performance. CFO needs to measure and monitor financial and operational business performance, analyze results, predict customers and plan for better business results.

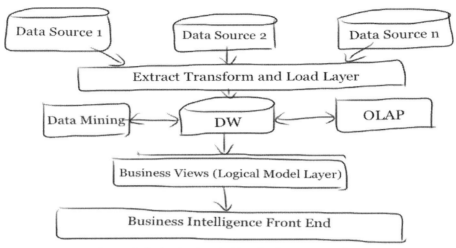

Sketch 3.5 A simple BI platform overview

Data Movement

With the explosive growth of unstructured data, and feasibility of big data analytics as a cloud service, the need to have a fast and reliable movement of huge data across any distance is increasing. There are various tools available in the market today that facilitate on premise data movement to the cloud. Majority of these tools use TCP based file transfer technology such as FTP or HTTP. TCP is unsuitable to the demands of today's big data applications. The TCP provides reliable data delivery under ideal conditions, but has an inherent throughput bottleneck that becomes obvious, and severe, with increased packet loss and latency found on long-distance WANs. Adding more bandwidth does not change the effective throughput. File transfer speeds do not improve and expensive bandwidth is underutilized. In local area networks with only a fraction of a percent packet loss, and on gigabit network, TCP's maximum throughput is only about 50 Mbps (5% bandwidth utilization). An FTP transfer across the United States over a link with 90ms latency and 1% packet loss has a maximum theoretical limit of 1.7 Mbps, independent of available bandwidth. On high-latency, high-loss intercontinental links or satellite networks, the effective throughput may be as low as 0.1% to 10% of available bandwidth. On a typical global link (3%/150ms), maximum TCP throughput degrades to 500-600 Kbps, utilizing only 5% of a 10 Mbps link.

In big data analytics use cases today, customer needs to move their large data to the cloud based storage before data can be loaded into a database or analytic warehouse. As TCP based data movement is not suitable for moving hundreds of terabyte data to the cloud storage, most cloud infrastructure provider offer a disk drive shipment service where customer needs to ship physical drives to the cloud provider data center. These drives are connected to the physical machines before data can be transferred. This introduces a lot of problems including loss of physical disks by shipping companies and a substantial delay in loading data.

Aspera is a software that facilitates movement of data using its patented protocol called FASP or Fast and secure protocol. FASP protocol eliminates the shortcomings of conventional TCP based file transfer technologies such as HTTP and FTP and facilitates data transfers at a speed at least hundred times than that of FTP/HTTP.

Features of FASP:

- Facilitates large data transfers at maximum speed
- Extremely lightweight, does not require any specialized hardware
- Provides control over the rate of transfer
- Automatic bandwidth capacity discovery between source and destination
- Provides end-to-end progress reporting of transfer
- Provides detailed performance statistics
- Includes complete built-in security
- Achieves reliability in application layer unlike TCP's inefficient loss and data handling

As an example of a file transfer using FASP, the following image shows the transfer rates and abilities of FASP and FTP. Evidently, FASP transfers 1GB file in 16 seconds whereas FTP takes over 6 minutes for the same. FASP makes good use of the available bandwidth for file transfers.

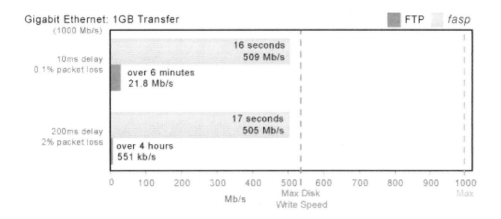

Fig: Comparison between FTP and FASP (Source: www.asperasoft.com)

Exercise

1. Install SQLite Add-ons for Firefox from:
   https://addons.mozilla.org/en-us/firefox/addon/sqlite-manager/
2. Create a sample schema with Employee, Department and Project tables.
3. Insert sample data
4. Try the queries learnt in this chapter

Questions

1. What are the two basic parts to a database table?
2. Suppose we are creating two tables. One, called ORDER_TABLE, will contain one row for each order taken by a company. Its primary key will be ORDER_NO. The second table is called ITEM_TABLE, and will contain one row for each item ordered (within an order a customer can order many items). Into which table should the foreign key be placed?
3. Which clauses in a SELECT statement are required?
4. If you reference multiple tables in the FROM clause, you should use JOIN conditions to obtain the desired result. - TRUE / FALSE
5. Which of the following situations applies if you forget the JOIN conditions in a SELECT statement using multiple tables:
   a. You receive an error and the statement is not executed.
   b. The statement is executed and the result is the Cartesian product of the tables.
6. Explain why query optimization is necessary.
7. What are the advantages of using indexes?
8. What are the disadvantages of using indexes?

9. How clustering of data can improve query performance?
10. What are the typical tasks provided by a database administrator?

Assignment

- Download DB2 Express C database:
  http://www-01.ibm.com/software/data/db2/express-c/download.html
- Create Sample database (use: db2sampl command)
- Run a sample query (use where clause and Group by)
- Generate query explain plan (use: db2exfmt tool)
- Post the query and db2exfmt output snapshot in a pdf document

Chapter

4

Big Data Analytics

Chapter Goal

After studying this chapter, you should be able to:

- Understand BigData and related technology
- Learn how to program with Hadoop and MapReduce framework
- Understand overview of Deep Question answer technology over text search

Introduction to BigData

The next challenge in front of us is what many experts characterize as the Big Data challenge; dealing with massive quantities of data, much of it unstructured. Organizations need to be able to handle uncertainty around format, velocity and change, particularly in some aspects of externally provided data. You think about social network information, trying to understand crowd sentiment and reaction. You think about what retailers go through, consumer packaged goods companies, automotive companies, anybody producing anything that they're pushing out to the consumer. You want to understand attitude, behavior, and reaction. You want to know your customers better. You want to create greater intimacy. You want to understand what they're feeling and thinking. The web, and todays interconnect environment, provides enormous opportunity for mining that data, getting at sentiment, the ability to handle data in real time and be able to deal with large quantities of unstructured data and unearth the patterns within. And then obviously, given size and scope, this is something that has to be workable and manageable by the average administrators.

What is Information stream?

Today's big data applications involve information arriving continuously over time in the form of data stream. In some cases, the rate and overall volume of data in the stream may be so big that it cannot all be stored for processing, and this leads to new requirements for efficiency and scalability. In other cases, the quantities of information may still be manageable, but the data stream perspective takes what has generally been a static view of a problem and adds a strong spatio temporal dimension to it.

Info stream is high-speed information flowing in real-time, often transient and not stored such as information flowing from sensors and other physical systems and instruments. The other few good examples are information flowing from real-time logs and activity monitors, streaming content like audio and video, and high speed transactions like tickers, trades, or traffic systems.

What is BigData?

There are many definitions of big data. Here's a useful one:

Small data is data that fits in-memory on a single desktop or machine with a capacity of between 1 GB and 10 GB of disk space.

Medium data fits on a single hard drive of 100 GB to 1 TB in size.

Large data is distributed over many machines, comprising 1 TB to multiple petabytes.

IDC estimates that in 2011, the amount of information created and replicated surpassed 1.8ZB (1.6 trillion gigabytes). Social interactions, mobile devices, facilities, equipment, R&D, simulations, and physical infrastructure all contribute to the flow.

In aggregate, this is called Big Data.

What do organizations want to do with big data?

Organizations including our government want to shift through unconventional information sources and find insights. They want to be able to access and gain insight into unconventional information as effectively as they do with operational, conventional information today. The pressure is to move towards more cost effective and flexible analytics and integrate the insights into infrastructure such as data warehouses, and enterprise applications. For example:

- Huge sets of governmental or publicly available data could help business optimizing their service offerings. According to a research report, one vacation resort drastically cut labor costs by syncing up its scheduling process with information from national weather service

- Business students at the University of Rochester used an IBM Watson to run predictive risk models on huge sets of government compliance information to narrow natural resource prospects.

- Manage natural disaster and outages - customers notify their provider of an outage, there may be other, real-time information coming in that could be linked in to refine response locations, times and problems. There may also be a jump in social media (tweet or Facebook updates) that could tip them off to a situation or details otherwise unknown to them while disconnected from customers.

- Get better demographic insight into how products and services are used by consumers. For example, a car dealership could take a more competitive stance with customers who have an eye on a van at a rival across the street with an extensive range of customer preferences and product details data.

Traditional approach to Analytics

Traditionally, data is collected from various heterogeneous sources in a company or business by a process commonly known as ETL; Extract Transform and Load. During the growth of departmental and enterprise data warehouses, there were many vendor tools came to market which promised end-to-end data acquisition and transformation that was much needed because of varied formats of data. Once extracted from Operational data store, transformed and loaded into a data warehouse, business analysis and reporting software helped data modeler and advanced business user generate nice reports for stakeholders and decision makers. Notice that in the figure below, even though data was coming from variety of sources within an enterprise, these sources were known. The most difficult part for any tool was to deal with the formats and transformation and cleansing of data.

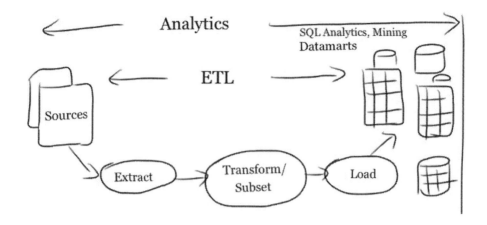

Sketch 4.1 Traditional Analytic Workflow

Emerging requirements for Analytics

The big data analytics requirement is evolving very rapidly. The explosive growth of information generated from mobile and real time sensors and surveillances is forcing a new set of low latency requirements that are now emerging.

- Telematics (Telecommunication and Informatics) and Mobile to mobile (M2M) apps are generating billions of records per second.
- Sophisticated cars, transport network and sensors generating billions of records per second.
- Real-time Cyber security monitoring / surveillance cameras are generating several million records per second.

There are several new requirements evident in the industry sectors. There is a need to collect and analyze many different sources and types of data generated by process control and instrumentation systems.

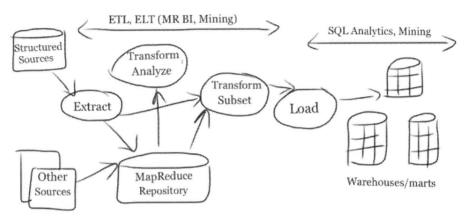

Sketch 4.2 Emerging requirements for analytics with scale and speed

Big Data Customer Use Cases

Big Data use case applies in every domain as it is all about smarter analytics based on all data, not just transactional data. Some domains have stronger and clearer use cases than the other but the tools and techniques (which is part of evolving BigData eco system) can be applied in all of the domain mentioned below

- Fraud detection in financial system
- Revenue assurance
- Healthcare outcome analysis
- Clinical trial outcome
- Churn analysis
- Web application optimization
- Advertising analysis
- Smart meter monitoring and prediction
- Warrantee management and prediction
- Equipment monitoring
- Legal discovery
- Pricing optimization
- Natural resource exploration
- Renewable energy sources placement and prediction
- Traffic flow optimization
- Weather forecasting

- Social network analysis
- IT infrastructure optimization
- Service delivery optimization
- Customer behavior analysis

Customer use case#1: Credit Cards Fraud detection

Use case scenario
Create critical data model elements, such as keys and transaction statistics, which feed real-time risk-scoring systems for fraud detection.

Requirement

Analyze volumes of data with response times that are not possible today, and apply analytic models to individual client, not just client segment. This requires building many more fraud detection models with much more data processing and much more detailed information.

A solution that is cost effective, fast, secure, flexible, reliable, and scalable. Warehouse solution is too expensive.

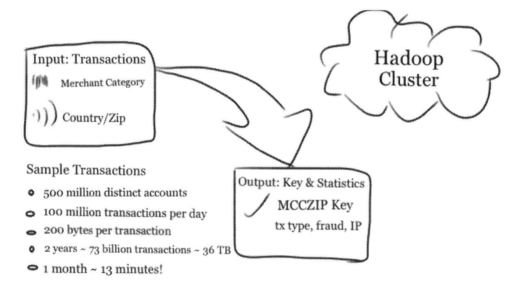

Sketch 4.3 Emerging requirements for analytics with scale and speed

Customer use case#2: Log Processing/Transaction error analytics

Use case scenario

A federated system of applications to provide account status and related information for customers. The federated application approach works very well in terms of ensuring near real time response to customers when they use the portal. There are occasions, however, when there are errors in transactions and customers call in with issues as soon as they occur.

Pain points

The current system of tracking these issues requires help desk analysts to look at the internal log portal and find out what happened. This usually takes about more than 24 hours to respond to the customer. The log portal depends on a system that collects log data from various application systems and aggregates them. The logs have different formats and correlating errors across applications can be tedious and error prone.   The bank tried to use a warehousing approach but could not succeed since the cost of such a solution was prohibitive and the response time demands could not be met.

Requirement

Need a cost-effective solution to reduce the response time to 2 minutes

Customer use case#3: Piracy of Video Streams

Use case scenario

MBC is facing a global increase in the unauthorized live streaming and re-broadcast of its content. These illegal sites allow users to either directly produce or watch live streaming video, link to other streaming sites, or share streams through P2P software. MBC also loses valuable content due to hijacking of any related comments, posts or conversations. Not only do these illegal sites represent a potential revenue loss but also a potential threat to MBC's overall business model and future growth. Although MBC knows these illegal sites exist, it does not have an analytical based assessment of how big the problem is, how the market is changing, how to quantify business impact or what the best options are to address this problem. They need the insights into the problem they have.

Requirement

- Analyze large volume of unstructured data
- Capture data from multiple sources and analyze the scope and potential impact of unauthorized streaming and deliver strategic recommendations on how to best confront theses pirating entities and overall trends.
- Know, how prevalent is the streaming of unauthorized content, what are the major URLs, platforms and where are these sites located? How are users discovering unauthorized content?
- Identify usage trends and factors that are driving consumer participation (e.g. sport, event, schedule, geographic location, access, etc.)?

Customer use case #4: Customer Acquisition and Retention

Use case scenario

GoodBuy has strong retail presence as brick and mortar business. They also have web presence. As retail economy is shifting towards web, GoodBuy needs to reconcile what they know about their customer's behavior in physical stores with web stores. They want to take action based on insights to enable new levels of customer services in both web and physical stores.

Requirement

- Weblog and click-stream analysis
- Integrated view between behavior data and transaction histories
- Competitive analysis

Customer use case#5: Sentiment Analysis for Products, Services and Brands

Scenario

Zapple releases a new tablet in USA and they are planning to release the product in emerging market in next few months. They want to monitor data from various sources such as blogs, boards, news feeds, tweets, and social media for information pertinent to brand and products, as well as competitors, so they can learn the lessons from USA launch and make the overseas launch even more successful.

Requirement

- Extract and aggregate relevant topics, relationships, discover patterns and reveal up-and-coming topics and trends

Sentiment Analysis – questions to ask

1. How do customers feel about our new advertising/ messages?
2. Is there any negative campaign chatter in social media that our public relation team should respond to?
3. What are the most talked about product attributes? What does it mean for customer support, new products development and potential acquisitions?
4. For my business, is consumer sentiment negatively impacting my business? Is our "brand hero" helping or hurting our reputation?
5. What is consumer sentiment regarding the product line we just launched?
6. What are the true competitive choices, we have? And what is emerging within?

Leveraging Big Data Analytics

The big challenge for businesses today is to deal with massive quantities of data, much of it unstructured. Businesses need to be able to handle uncertainty around format, velocity and change, particularly in some aspects of externally provided data. You think about social network information. You think about trying to understand crowd sentiment and reaction. You think about what retailers go through, consumer packaged goods companies, automotive companies, anybody producing anything that they're pushing out to the consumer. You want to understand attitude, behavior, and reaction. You want to know your customers better. You want to create greater intimacy. You want to understand what they're feeling and thinking. The web, and todays interconnect environment, provides enormous opportunity for mining that data, getting at sentiment, but does require the ability to handle data in real time and be able to deal with large quantities of unstructured data and unearth the patterns and the embedded information contained within that data. And then obviously, given size and scope, this is something that has to be workable and manageable by your average administrators. The sketch below illustrates the proposed framework to handle big data challenge for the competitive advantages. There are plenty of Hadoop based Analytic platforms in the market today. IBM offers a comprehensive Big Data platform called IBM Infosphere BigInsight, which is enabling modern IT to take on the BigData challenges and get most out of them.

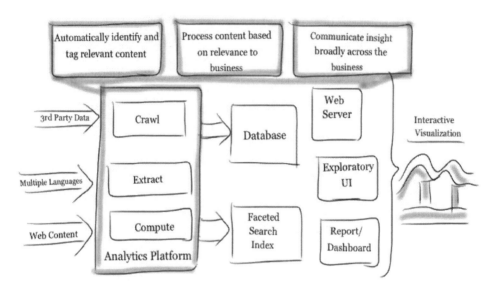

Sketch 4.4 BigData Analytic Platform

Watson & Power of Big Data Analytics

Think about it for a second: what would a machine have to do to replicate what a human does when we answer questions? It turns out, quite a bit: first the person must hear the question and process what he/she hears into concepts that can be understood or natural language processing, in computer parlance. Then the person must consult their stored knowledge to see if they can find enough information to either make an educated guess or not. Once the person has determined their level of confidence in their answer, they need to decide if they are confident enough to ring in and put some money on the line. At that point the person, if they decide to ring in, must process their answer into speech--and frame that speech, in Jeopardy's (America's most favorite quiz show: http://www.jeopardy.com/) case, into a question.

Open-Domain Q&A

An open domain QA takes rich natural language questions over a broad domain of knowledge and delivers:

- Precise Answers: Determine what is being asked & give precise response
- Accurate Confidences: Determine likelihood answer is correct
- Consumable Justifications: Explain why the answer is right
- Fast Response Time: Precision & Confidence in <3 seconds

Keyword Evidence in Q&A

In Question Answer domain, we face a lot of technical challenges but the most challenging part is to deal with the many ways you can express the same meaning. Natural Language (NL) is often very sensitive to context and is often incomplete, tacit and ambiguous. Simplified approaches can lead you astray. Consider the question below:

In May 1898 Portugal celebrated the 400th anniversary of this explorer's arrival in India.

The systems parses it into is logical structure – things centered on the predicate celebrated etc. Now consider that based on keywords it would be straight-forward to pick up this potentially answer-bearing passage:

In May, Gary arrived in India after he celebrated his anniversary in Portugal

This is a great hit from a Keyword search perspective and by that score gives good evidence that **Gary** is the answer. And it might be but of course in this case – **Gary** is not the answer, -- Vasco De Gama is the answer.

The system must learn that of all sorts of evidence different algorithms might produce, some evidence under some conditions is stronger than other evidence. Using probabilistic machine learning algorithms, it has to learn this automatically.

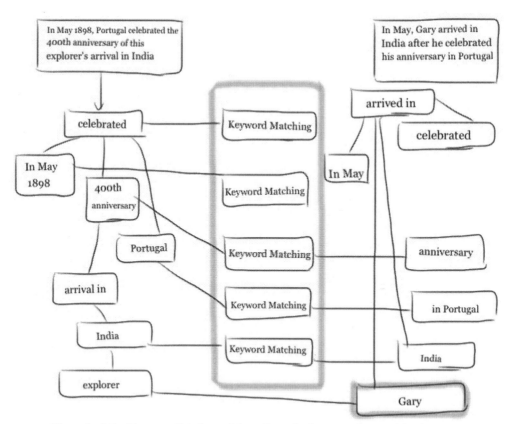

Sketch 4.5 Expert Q&A vs. Text Search (keyword matching)

Deeper Evidences

Here we see the same question, the same parse, but on the other side we see that there exists a passage containing the RIGHT answer BUT with only one key word in common.

On the 27th of May 1498, Vasco da Gama landed in Kappad Beach

The system must consider in parallel and in detail a huge amount of content just to get a SHOT at this evidence and then must find and weigh the right inferences that will allow it to match and score with an accurate confidence, for example in this case system performed Date Time (Temporal) reasoning, statistical paraphrasing and Geospatial reasoning. And its still not 100% certain. What if, for example, the passage said "considered landing in" rather than "landed in" or what if there was just a preponderance of weaker evidence for another answer. Question Answering Technology tries to understand what the user is really asking for and to deliver precise and correct responses. But Natural language is hard.

Meaning can be expressed in so many different ways and to achieve high levels of precision and confidence you must consider much more information and analyze it much more deeply. Here we need a radically different approach that explores many different plaussive interpretations in parallel and collects and evaluates all sorts of evidence in support or in refutation of those possibilities.

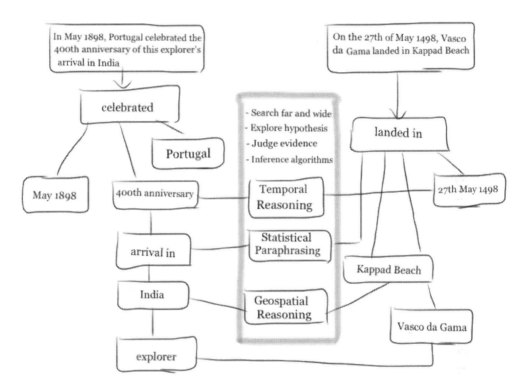

Sketch 4.6 Expert Q&A vs. Text Search (Deep QA technology)

Big Data Technology Overview

From technology perspective, big data is all about Hadoop and an eco-system around it. However it is important to note that columnar database technology and information streaming technology are playing a big role in big data analytics.

Apache Hadoop distributed file system (HDFS)

HDFS is a distributed file system designed to run on commodity hardware. It has many similarities with existing distributed file systems but differences are significant. HDFS is highly fault tolerant and optimized for large data sets. It is built for batch processing on BigData. HDFS is optimized to support very large files that typically range in size from megabytes to terabytes. It's best to have a relatively modest number of these large files than to have a large number of smaller files. You should note that HDFS intentionally relaxed support for certain POSIX standards to achieve its performance goals.

HDFS is designed for streaming data access. At load time, HDFS automatically spreads data across nodes in the cluster to facilitate parallel processing of that data at read time. Unlike many traditional file systems, HDFS is designed to minimize the time required to read an entire data set rather than the time required to read the first record or a small subset of the data. Thus, HDFS isn't suitable for applications that require low-latency data access; instead, it's designed to provide efficient, batch access to large volumes of data. HDFS has a simple concurrency model that presumes data will be written once (by one writer) and read many times by various applications. There is no support for multiple concurrent writers or for updating a subset of data at an arbitrary point within a file.

As mentioned before, HDFS was designed to provide fault tolerance for Hadoop. By default, data blocks (i.e., portions of a file) are replicated across multiple nodes at load or write time. The degree of replication is configurable; the default is to replicate across 3 nodes. Replication of data helps Hadoop recover from hardware failures that can periodically occur when using large clusters of low-cost commodity hardware.

HDFS Architecture – Master/Slaves

In Hadoop terminology, *node = machine*

HDFS consists of a master node (hosting the NameNode, which manages meta data about the file system) and a collection of slave nodes or data nodes (which store portions of files). In the sketch above, a client application wanting to read data issues requests that the master node or name node resolves. The name node communicates with the data nodes to obtain the necessary information, and the data nodes return this information to the client. Here we see that a rack typically consists of multiple data nodes, and each data node manages multiple blocks of data. As I mentioned earlier, data blocks are replicated across multiple nodes to provide for fault tolerance.

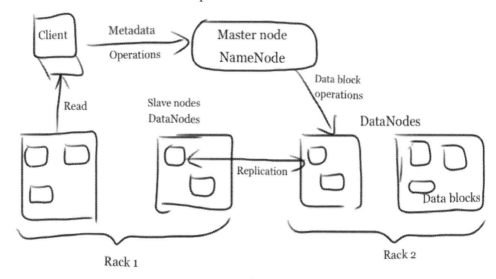

Sketch 4.7 Master-Slave architecture of Hadoop file system

HDFS – NameNode

The NameNode manages the file system namespace, allowing clients to work with files and directory subtrees. HDFS supports a traditional hierarchical file organization. A user or an application can create directories and store files inside these directories. The file system namespace hierarchy is similar to most other existing file systems; one can create and remove files, move a file from one directory to another, or rename a file. The NameNode maintains the file system namespace. Any change to the file system namespace or its properties is recorded by the NameNode.

The NameNode maintains two persistent files (a namespace image and edit log), both of which I'll discuss later. However, metadata about what blocks of data reside on which Data Nodes is loaded into memory at start up time, when new DataNodes join a cluster, and periodically thereafter. Of course, the metadata size is limited to the RAM available on the NameNode. Since lots of small files would require more metadata than a small number of large files, the in-memory metadata management issue explains why HDFS favors the latter over the former. If a NameNode runs out of RAM, it will crash and applications won't be able to use HDFS until the NameNode is online again.

Indeed, the NameNode is an essential component of HDFS, and a loss of this node will render the file system inaccessible. Because of this, the NameNode represents a single point of failure for Hadoop, so administrators must take care to make this node resistant to failure. A little later, I'll describe some techniques for doing that. By the way, a future release of Hadoop may introduce a BackupNameNode for hot standby capabilities.

The NameNode is responsible for managing metadata associated with each block in the HDFS. As the amount of information in the rack scales into the 10's or 100's of TB, this can grow to be quite sizable. The NameNode machine needs to keep the blockmap in RAM to work efficiently. Therefore, at large scale, this machine will require more RAM than other machines in the cluster. The amount of metadata can also be dropped almost in half by doubling the block size:

```
<property>
<name>dfs.block.size</name>
<value>134217728</value>
</property>
```

HDFS - DataNode (Slave)

DataNodes manage names and locations of file blocks, which are 64MB each by default. For large files, you may want to increase the block since to 128MB. Doing so decreases pressure on the NameNode's memory. On the other hand, this potentially decreases the amount of parallelism that can be achieved, as the number of blocks per file decreases. This means fewer hosts may have sections of a file to offer to MapReduce tasks without contending for disk access. The larger the individual files involved (or the more files involved in the average MapReduce job), the less of an issue this is.

HDFS uses data blocks to help provide for fault tolerance and reliability. By default, HDFS replicates each data block to 3 different nodes, including 1 node that resides on a separate rack. If a disk or node fails, Hadoop can seamlessly transfer work to an online node that contains a copy of the data. The details of HDFS's storage subsystem are transparent to users. In particular, application programmers don't need to manually decompose files into blocks and distribute these across nodes in the cluster. And the NameNode handles file system meta data separately from DataNodes, which manage the data blocks.

HDFS – Datablocks

HDFS Datablocks are much larger than traditional file system blocks. A typical block size is 64MB. If chunk of file is smaller than HDFS block size, only needed space is used. Map tasks in MapReduce normally operate on one block at a time so if you have too few tasks (fewer than nodes in the cluster), your jobs will run slower than they could otherwise

The main advantages of HDFS's data block approach are that it simplifies replication, providing fault tolerance and reliability and shields users from storage subsystem details.

Reliability & Datablock Replication

Each datablock is replicated across 3 DataNodes (by default)

- 1st replica placed on same node as client
- 2nd replica placed on different rack from 1st rack
- 3rd replica placed on same rack as 2nd rack, but on a different node and striped

Hadoop uses data replication to promote reliability and fault tolerance. By default, each data block is replicated across 3 nodes. (A configuration parameter enables users to change the replication factor.) Let's talk briefly about Hadoop's replication strategy.

HDFS attempts to place the first replica on the same node as the client if the client is running on the cluster. If the client isn't running on the cluster, the first replica is placed on a random node – one that doesn't appear too busy or full. HDFS places the second replica is placed on a different rack from the replica. The selected rack is randomly chosen. Finally, HDFS places the third replica on the same rack as the second replica, but on a different node (chosen at random). The idea here is to balance several competing objectives:

- Reliability (achieved by storing copies of the same block on 2 different racks)
- Write bandwidth (writes traverse only 1 network switch)
- Read bandwidth (a given block can be read from 2 different racks)
- Block distribution across the cluster (a client executing on the cluster only writes a single block on its local rack)

NameNode High Availability (HA)

Prior to Hadoop 2.0.0, NameNode was a single-point-of-failure in an HDFS cluster. If the name node in HDFS failed, the cluster as a whole would become unavailable until the name node was restarted or brought up on a different machine. In the later releases, Hadoop comes with High Availability of the NameNode. This is achieved by running two redundant name nodes in the Active/Passive configuration with a hot standby. Two separate machines are configured as the name node and at any point of time, only one of the machine is in Active State while the other stays in Standby State. The data nodes are configured with the location of both the name nodes and they send block location information and heartbeats to both name nodes. This allows the standby node to have up-to-date information and a fast failover when the active name node crashes.

Data Replication Pipeline

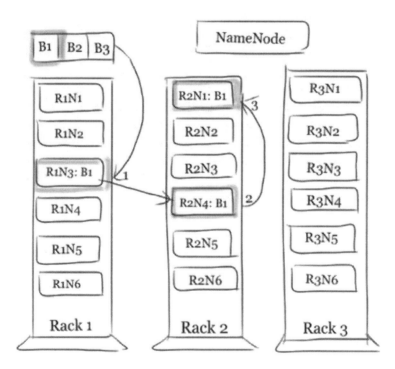

Sketch 4.8 Data replication in HDFS

On the sketch above, you see a Hadoop cluster with three racks. Each rack contains multiple nodes, represented by rectangular boxes. For example, on the far left you'll see a box labeled R1N1, which represents Node 1 on Rack 1. For simplicity, each rack shown here has 6 nodes. At top, you see the NameNode, which we discussed earlier. When the client application attempts to write a new file to HDFS, the NameNode will perform various checks to make sure that the client has appropriate security authorization to do so, that the file doesn't already exist, and so on. Assuming all goes well, the client can write the file to an output stream, which HDFS will break into pieces and distribute across the cluster. The NameNode allocates new blocks for the data and selects the nodes on which to store the replicas.

Let's follow the path of one particular data block – block B1 on this chart. B1 is first written to Node 3 on Rack 1. A copy is then written on a different rack – Rack 2, in this case. In fact, it's written to Node 4 on Rack 2. The third and final copy of the block is written to the same rack as the second copy – Rack 2 – but a different node (Node 1, in this example).

Data Replication Pipeline#2

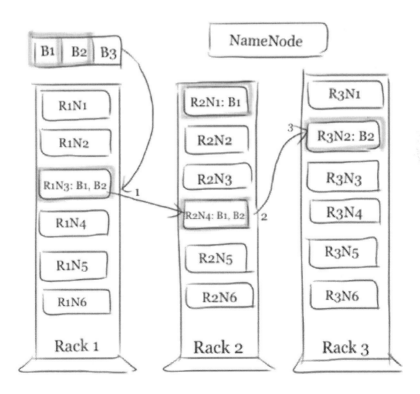

Sketch 4.9   Data replication in HDFS

Let's follow the path of one particular data block – block B1, shown on this
sketch. B1 is first written to Node 4 on Rack 1. A copy is then written on a
different rack – Rack 2, in this case. In fact, it's written to Node 4 on Rack 2.
The third and final copy of the block is written to the same rack as the second
copy – Rack 2 – but a different node.

Data Replication Pipeline#3

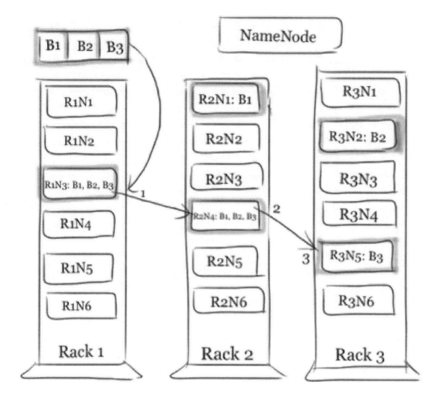

Sketch 4.10   Data replication in HDFS

Recovery using Replication

The NameNode exploits data block replication to recover from DataNode
failures. DataNodes periodically send "heartbeat" checks to the NameNode to
let the NameNode know that they're online. If the NameNode doesn't receive
a heartbeat from a particular DataNode, it marks that node as dead and stops
forwarding any new I/O requests to that DataNode. Effectively, it considers

any data registered to that node to be "lost." To recover the lost data, the NameNode consults its in-memory metadata to determine which data blocks were managed by the node. It locates other DataNodes that have copies of these blocks and directs I/O requests to an online DataNode that has a replica of the lost data. It also instructs these DataNodes to copy the "lost" blocks to other nodes whenever possible.

Cluster maintenance – Rebalancing

To maintain good data distribution across a cluster, rebalancing is sometimes needed. For example, if you add a new DataNode to the cluster, HDFS won't automatically copy any data blocks from existing files to it. As you write new files to HDFS, it will distribute data across active DataNodes, including those that you may have recently added. But this still means that "new" nodes won't have as much local data as "old" nodes. Consequently, to achieve maximum parallelization of work when running MapReduce jobs, Hadoop may attempt to copy more data blocks from "old" nodes to the "new" node. Doing so increases network bandwidth, which may be an acceptable price to pay for the added parallelization. However, if you use the HDFS Balancer utility on a regular basis or after adding new DataNodes, you can avoid consuming unnecessary network bandwidth at runtime because Hadoop won't need to copy blocks from one node to another.

Map Reduce Programming Paradigm

Hadoop MapReduce is a software framework for writing applications which process vast amounts of data (multi-terabyte data-sets) in-parallel on large clusters (thousands of nodes) of commodity hardware in a reliable, fault-tolerant manner.

A MapReduce job usually splits the input data-set into independent chunks that are processed by the map tasks in a completely parallel manner. The framework sorts the outputs of the maps, which are then input to the reduce tasks. Typically both the input and the output of the job are stored in a file-system. The framework takes care of scheduling tasks, monitoring them and re-executes the failed tasks. MapReduce is great for loosely coupled parallelization tasks. It is not well suited to situations where tight coupling (message passing or shared memory, or large graph processing algorithms). It also does better where the amount of computation required is significantly more than any one computer.

For example, you have 10,000 source files that are relatively independent of one another (e.g. you don't have cross file references to resolve), and processing each file takes one minute. On a single computer, this would take 7 days to process. With a MapReduce cluster of 100 machines, it would take about 2 hours.

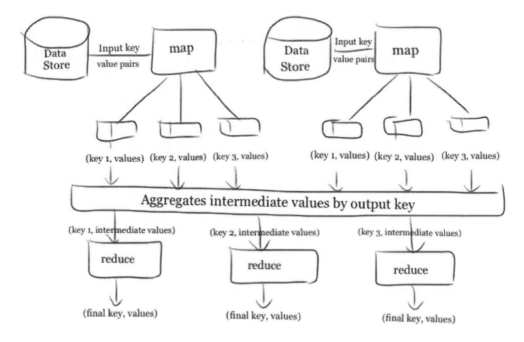

Sketch 4.11 MapReduce programming model

Here's a graphical representation of the MapReduce programming model. At the upper half on the chart, you'll see two sets of data, presumably on two different nodes. Two map tasks operate over their respective data sets, consuming key/value pairs extracted from the data, performing any necessary processing, and generating new key/value pairs as output. The system sorts the keys and groups each unique key with all its values. That work is shown in the middle of this chart. The aggregated output keys are sent to various reduce tasks, which in turn perform additional processing and output final values back to the client application.

Map step: The master node takes the input, chops it up into smaller sub-problems, and distributes those to worker nodes. A worker node may do this again in turn, leading to a multi-level tree structure. The worker node processes that smaller problem, and passes the answer back to its master node.

Reduce step: The master node then takes the answers to all the sub-problems and combines them in some way to get the output - the answer to the problem it was originally trying to solve.

MapReduce – Job Execution

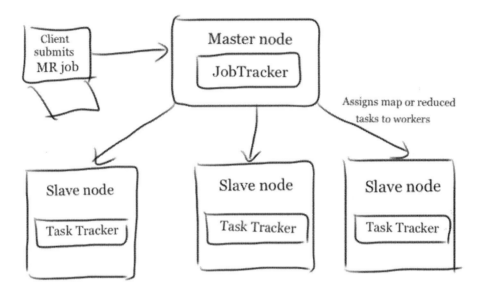

Sketch 4.12   MapReduce job execution

First, a client submits a MapReduce job (or application) to the JobTracker. The JobTracker is a process running on a master node. The JobTracker takes this job, breaks into pieces (or tasks), and assigns work to TaskTrackers running on various slave nodes.

MapReduce – Job Execution (behind the scenes)

Well, a single job (or application) consists of an unordered set of "Map" tasks that have a locality preference. That means that Hadoop favors executing map tasks close to where the data for that task resides. Whenever possible, a node that contains a copy of the data to be processed is given the associated map task to perform. If this isn't possible – perhaps the node is offline or busy – the JobTracker tries to assign the task to a node in the same rack as the data. Reduce tasks are also unordered sets. I already mentioned how tasks are scheduled by the JobTracker and executed by individual TaskTrackers. There is

1 Task Tracker per node, and each TaskTracker has a fixed number of "slots" for Map and Reduce tasks. This number can vary from node to node. The TaskTracker periodically communicates with the JobTracker to indicate that it's alive and to report on the number of free slots available on its node for new tasks.

MapReduce HDFS Co-located

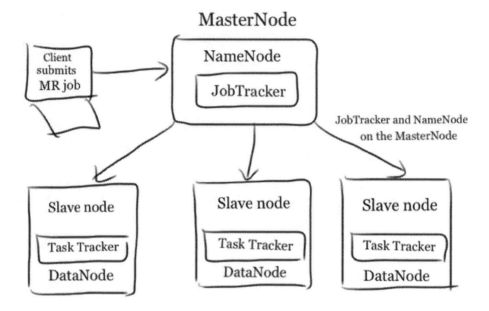

Sketch 4.13 MapReduce job execution model collocated with HDFS

You might be wondering how MapReduce processes relate to HDFS nodes in a cluster. Here is one possible configuration. The JobTracker and NameNode share the same node in this topology, although that doesn't necessarily need to be the case. The slave nodes store and manage HDFS data – i.e., they are DataNodes – and run MapReduce tasks as directed –i.e., they support the TaskTracker process.

Fault Tolerance

Let's talk a little bit about fault tolerance from a MapReduce point of view. Task processes send "heartbeat" checks to their TaskTrackers. If a task doesn't send a heartbeat within 10 minutes, the TaskTracker presumes that it's dead and kills the task's JVM. It also reports the failed task to the JobTracker. The

JobTracker will then reschedule the task, typically on a different node with a different TaskTracker. If a TaskTracker reports a high number of failed tasks, the JobTracker will blacklist it to prevent the node from blocking the entire job. In addition, if a TaskTracker fails to send regular heartbeat checks to the JobTracker (by default, every 10 minutes), the JobTracker will presume that it has failed.

Apache Hive

Hive is a data warehousing infrastructure based on the Hadoop. Hadoop provides massive scale out and fault tolerance capabilities for data storage and processing on commodity hardware. Hive was initially developed by Facebook. Hive provides a distributed data warehouse infrastructure that runs on top of Hadoop. Hive is basically intuitive and simplistic abstraction on top of Hadoop to access data from hdfs. . Internally hive uses map reduce for processing of big data. Hive is **NOT** designed for online transaction processing and does not offer real-time queries and row level updates. It is best used for batch jobs over large sets of immutable data (like web logs).

Hive architecture

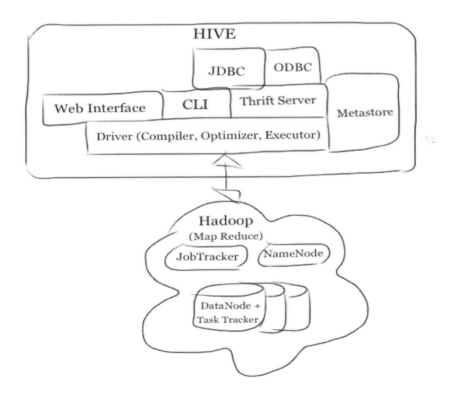

Sketch 4.14   Hive architecture

The sketch above shows the major components of hive. Hive provides CLI and web based external interfaces. Hive also supports API based interfaces such as JDBC and ODBC. Thrift server provides a simple client API to execute hiveQL. Hive metastore is a system catalog, a central repository of all hive metadata. The metadata is created during table creation and reused every time a table is accessed or referenced.

Data Units in Hive

Databases are Namespaces that separate tables and other data units from naming confliction.

Tables are Homogeneous units of data, which have the same schema. Each table is stored in a corresponding HDFS directory. Data in the table is stored in files within that directory.

When a table is created in hive, data is moved to hive warehouse by default. You can also create an external table in hive. Creating an external table will tell hive to refer the data at an existing location rather than moving the data within hive warehouse. When you drop a hive managed table, the data and its metadata both are deleted. In case of an external table drop, only the metadata is deleted, the original data is left untouched.

Here question arises which type of hive table one shall choose. Choosing a table type is just a matter of user's preference. However, just a rule of thumb could be that if you plan to use same dataset across hive and other tools, it is wise to create an external table. Using external table also gives you facility to associate multiple schemas with same dataset.

Partitions

Each hive table can have one or more partitions. Partitions are basically storage units. Apart from being storage units, partitions also facilitate to efficiently identify the rows satisfying a query criterion. Take an example of system log files which has a timestamp associated with each log record. We can partition the records in log file according to date. This would help in searching a log record based on a particular date since it only scans the partitions that the query requires. Partitions are defined while creating a hive table using PARTITIONED BY clause.

Buckets

Data in each partition may in turn be divided into Buckets based on the value of a hash function of some column of the Table. This gives an extra structure to the data, which in turn would facilitate query execution.

Example

hive> **CREATE TABLE logs(t1 string, t2 string, t3 string, t4 string, t5 string,) ROW FORMAT DELIMITED FIELDS TERMINATED BY ' ';**

hive> **LOAD DATA LOCAL INPATH 'sample.log' OVERWRITE INTO TABLE logs;**

hive> **SELECT t4 AS sev, COUNT(*) AS cnt FROM logs WHERE t4 LIKE '[%' GROUP BY t4;**

Hive provides a query language called hive QL which is very similar to standard ANSI SQL. This makes it easy for anyone to query big data stored in HDFS. It provides the following operations with the ability to:

- filter rows from a table using a where clause.
- select certain columns from the table using a select clause.
- do equi-joins between two tables.
- evaluate aggregations on multiple "group by" columns for the data stored in a table.
- store the results of a query into another table.
- download the contents of a table to a local (e.g., nfs) directory.
- store the results of a query in a hadoop dfs directory.
- manage tables and partitions (create, drop and alter).
- plug in custom scripts in the language of choice for custom map/reduce jobs.

Apache HBase

HBase is a column-oriented database management system that runs on top of HDFS. HBase is well suited when you need random, real time access to your big data. HBase is an open-source, distributed, versioned, column-oriented store, which is modeled after Google's Bigtable. Just as Bigtable leverages the distributed data storage provided by the Google File System, Apache HBase provides Bigtable-like capabilities on top of HDFS. HBase is most suited for a very large data set. HBase provides fast lookup of records from large datasets stored on HDFS. Internally HBase stores your data in indexed "StoreFiles" which resides on HDFS for high speed data lookup. HBase master handles the load balancing of regions across the region server.

Exercise

Twitter Sentiment analysis using Python

Social media tools such as Twitter has become a hub where people voluntarily express their opinions across any topic imaginable. And the result is a large number of tweets being produced every second. This data source is incredibly valuable for researchers, analysts and businesses. For example, researchers and data scientists are using tweets to predict stock market based on people's mood drawn from their posts/communications on twitter.

Exercise 1: Query Twitter data using Python scripting language

This tutorial walks through a MapReduce implementation using Python programming language. In this exercise you will retrieve recent tweets for a given keyword such as "BigData".

- Access the twitter Application Programming Interface (API) using python.
- Estimate the public's perception (the sentiment) of a particular term or phrase.
- Analyze the relationship between location and mood based on a sample of twitter data.

This example uses famous word count problem. And uses a simple data input file. You can also make use of literature text sources - Shakespeare's complete works and Mark Twain's Huckleberry Finn. These and many others works are available at Project Gutenberg (www.gutenberg.org). Students are encouraged to find and use alternate text sources that are interesting to them, even if they're not available at Project Gutenberg.

Map Reduce exercise without Hadoop

- Setup Python on your computer.
- Copy python program **wordcount.py** and sample input data file **Huckleberry.txt** from Book chapter4 directory from box.net

- Also download MapReduce.py from the same book website and copy in the same place where wordcount.py resides.
- Run as **python wordcount.py wordcount.txt**

Read the mapper and reducer function in wordcount.py and make sure you understand it well. This should give students basic understanding of solving problem using MapReduce programming paradigm. Now, move on to running mapper and reducer functions on Hadoop file system.

Map Reduce exercise in Hadoop

1. Setup single node Hadoop cluster on Ubuntu Linux
   - Setup Java
   - Add a dedicated Hadoop system user
   - Configure SSH for managing nodes
   - Disable IPv6
   - Install Hadoop

2. Copy python program **mapper.py, reducer.py** and sample input data files **shakespeare.txt** and **huckleberry.txt** from Book chapter4 directory from box.net
3. Test your mapper and reducer program locally without running them as a MapReduce job:

```
echo "we can do everything that we think we should do" |
python /home/ranjanr/mapper.py

cat /home/ranjanr/Shakespeare.txt | python
/home/ranjanr/mapper.py | sort -k1,1
```

4. Once tested then you can move on to copy the input data to HDFS data directory `hadoop dfs -copyFromLocal /tmp/data /home/ranjanr/data`
5. Run the MapReduce job as below

```
hadoop jar contrib/streaming/hadoop-*streaming*.jar \
-file /home/ranjanr/mapper.py    -mapper
/home/ranjanr/mapper.py \
-file /home/ranjanr/reducer.py    -reducer
/home/ranjanr/reducer.py \
-input /home/ranjanr/data/* -output /home/ranjanr/data-
output
```

Chapter

5

Network Protocols & Services

Chapter Goal

After studying this chapter, you should be able to:

- evaluate technical descriptions of communication protocols and demonstrate your understanding of their operation
- describe the role played by primitives in the OSI reference model
- describe the main functions of the principal protocols in the TCP/IP architecture

Introduction

A network is a group of connected, communicating devices. An **internet** is a two or more network that can communicate with each other. The most notable internet is called the **Internet**. Millions of people are users. Yet this extraordinary communication system only came into being in 1969.

In early 80s, researchers started designing specifications for a single physical network that can carry both voice and data traffic. This led to the publication of the requirements for an integrated services digital network (ISDN) in 1988. The idea of ISDN was to divide the traffic into specific categories, called services, according to the communication requirements of the data: for example, the type of data, the transfer mode and the transfer rate. An ISDN is an example of a *multi-service network*, which can be loosely defined as a network that provides a range of services over a common transport mechanism – that is, a common means of transferring data between devices.

The Internet may be regarded as another example of a multi-service network, although the quality of service may not meet users' requirements for some applications. Private networks that operate to the same specification as the Internet can offer users a better quality of service, and the network operators can exercise greater control over the traffic. Such networks are called **intranets**.

Delivering data over network

In traditional telephone networks, a reserved transmission path is established between terminals before the users can talk to each other. Typically, the transmission path is capable of transmitting at a data rate of 64 kilobit/sec simultaneously in both directions. Because only one person usually talks at any one time and there are natural gaps in conversation, over half the transmission capacity is wasted. However, because the transmission path is reserved, once a connection is established there is no queuing delay waiting for resources to become available. In addition, the end-to-end delay is constant because, once a path is set up; it does not change throughout a call. For voice traffic it is important that any delay in transport is constant as well as being as small as possible. The transfer mode in which a path is reserved exclusively for a single communication is called **circuit switching.**

The requirement for a constant delay was not important in the early computer applications, and this encouraged the development of packet switching. In **packet switching** the message to be sent is divided into convenient groups of data, called packets, which are transferred independently over the network. Transmission capacity is not reserved. Instead, at each stage through the network, if transmission capacity is not available to send a packet immediately, the packet is stored until sufficient capacity becomes available, at which point it is forwarded on to the next stage. Since capacity is not reserved for specific paths between users, if there are idle periods in the transmission of packets between two users, that capacity is available to other users and is not wasted.

In most cases, packet switching is more efficient than circuit switching at using transmission capacity, and it can be more resilient to network failures and congestion. For instance, if a switch detects that a link has become faulty; packets can be diverted to another link without any intervention by the users and without their knowledge. In circuit switching, if a link develops a fault, the transmission of data must be stopped and the circuit re-established. Although re-establishment may be performed automatically and very quickly, it may result in loss of data.

Internetwork

An internetwork is a network of networks, composed of terminals, switches and communication media. The overall objective of an internetwork is to allow communication between two (or more) networks. In large internetworks, communication between systems is a complicated process, and to cope with this complexity the hardware and software in the systems are organized as a hierarchy of layers. Each layer performs some of the functions necessary to achieve communication between systems. The layers, particularly higher layers, are mostly implemented as software components of communication networks. It is very important to understand and appreciate the hierarchical nature of communication systems: each layer, except the lowest, is built upon the layer below. The layered separation of functions can also be seen in everyday examples, such as sending a letter. You write a letter to a friend and enclose it in an envelope with the address written on it. You then post the letter and wait for it to be delivered. You don't give precise instructions about how the letter is to be delivered and what to do if unusual events occur. You leave these sorts of tasks to the postal service – the lower layers. The postal workers should not be interested in the contents of your letter – only the address written on the envelope – and your letter should be delivered with the contents unchanged, that is, free from error. The postal workers will decide the best route for your letter. This may involve carrying the letter by road, rail, sea or air but all this is irrelevant to you (although it may affect the cost of postage and can be considered as part of a quality-of-service agreement). Within the postal service the functions may be divided further. The local postal workers may be interested only in parts of the address to decide to which country or town your letter should be forwarded. Within a town, the postal code or street name may be important to allocate your letter to the appropriate delivery round. Perhaps your friend has moved addresses and has told the postal service to forward their mail to a new address; the postal service would take care of this too. You can see that you and the postal workers are operating at different levels of abstraction. You may find it helpful to create your own analogies of layering.

A layer can be thought of as providing services to the layer above. How these services are achieved is not the concern of the higher layer: it needs to know how to interact with the services, but not how they are implemented. The specification of the interface between two layers is very important because the equipment implementing the layers may be produced by different manufacturers. In providing services, a layer may perform several important functions. For instance, it is very convenient if the transfer of data can be considered to be free from transmission error. However, transmission errors do occur, and in some media they occur relatively frequently. It greatly simplifies the design of software if one layer performs the functions necessary to detect and correct transmission errors, thereby allowing all higher layers to assume that the transmission is free from this type of error.

Internet Standards & Administration

The Internet has evolved and gained a broader user base with significant commercial activity. Various groups that coordinate Internet issues have guided this growth and development:

- Internet Society (ISOC) http://www.isoc.org/
- Internet Architecture Board (IAB) http://www.iab.org/
- Internet Engineering Task Force (IETF) http://www.ietf.org/
- Internet Research Task Force (IRTF) http://irtf.org/
- Internet Assigned Numbers Authority (IANA) http://www.iana.org/
- Names and Numbers (ICANN) http://www.icann.org/
- Network Information Center (NIC) http://www.internic.net/

Internet Name Architecture

The Internet is divided into domains, and an authority in each domain is responsible for allocating names. However, the domains may be divided into sub-domains and the responsibility of allocating sub-domain names may be delegated to other authorities. In this way the names form a tree structure as shown in sketch below. The Internet Assigned Number Authority (IANA) has overall responsibility for assigning domain names on the Internet.

What is a protocol?

A service normally requires some communication between systems in a communication network, and the set of rules that govern the communication is called *a* **protocol**. These rules are expressed in terms of the format of messages exchanged between two systems (the syntax), and the way in which the messages should be interpreted (the semantics). In this context, a protocol determines how communication takes place between the same layers in different systems, that is, between peer layers, and for this reason you may see this type of communication referred to as peer-to-peer. The peer layers exchange data as though there is a direct link between the two but in reality all the data is passed down through all the layers and is carried by the physical media in the form of signals. It is very important to have open and internationally agreed protocols that enable widely different types of equipment to interact with each other.

The Open Systems Interconnection (OSI) Reference Model

In 1978 the International Organization for Standardization (ISO) defined a framework for describing the layers in communication networks, called the Open Systems Interconnection (OSI) reference model. Although many networks may not fit the strict definition of the model and the model has been modified with the introduction of sub-layers, the OSI reference model does provide a very good framework for discussing communication networks.

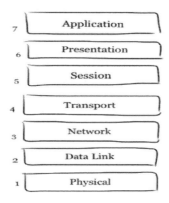

Sketch 5.1 OSI layer

The OSI reference model has seven layers:

Physical layer – provides the mechanical, electrical and procedural means for transmitting bits over a communication medium.

Data link layer – provides services for the transmission of data between directly connected systems in a communication network.

Network layer – handles the routing of data through communication networks.

Transport layer – provides reliable end-to-end services without being concerned about the route through communication networks.

Session layer – provides facilities to organize and synchronize dialogues, i.e. communications that consist of several strands such as audio and video components.

Presentation layer – deals with issues about how data is represented and ensures that the systems agree on how the information is transferred.

Application layer – provides the means for application programs to access the communication system represented by the OSI reference model. For instance, the application layer can provide services for supporting file transfer and email.

The lowest three layers are primarily concerned with the problems of transferring data across physical networks, and the highest four layers are associated with end-to-end issues and not the specific details of any communication network. Intermediate systems in Figure 5 are shown as pairs of stacks of layers. Different conditions may be encountered on the two sides of an intermediate system: for instance, different transmission media may link two systems together.

Level of Abstraction

The physical layer deals with the practicalities of transmitting data over a physical medium and hides these from the data link layer. So from the data link layer's viewpoint transmitting data takes the form of sending 1s and 0s.

The data link layer may have to deal with errors occurring during transmission and with complications that arise from sharing a transmission medium. These problems are hidden from the network layer.

From the network layer's viewpoint a network sends blocks of data between switches, but these blocks may be lost or reordered. The network layer navigates the blocks of data through the network(s) and hides these complications from the transport layer.

The transport layer does not need to know about the physical structure, or architecture, of the network(s). It views a network as a direct channel between two users for transporting data. The session layer does not always take any actions associated with the transport of data, but it may have to enhance the services of the transport layer in order to fulfill user requirements. For instance, a session may involve a sequence of independent transactions. The presentation layer provides communication services to users about how certain information is represented, such as dates and people's names. The application layer deals with specific classes of applications and may involve the identification of users.

TCP/IP Layer

The *Internet* is a worldwide public internetwork, which allows computers to communicate with each other even though they may have different manufacturers and different operating systems. The origins of the Internet lie in a project of the US Defense Advanced Research Project Agency in the 1970s, where it was intended to foster communication between research institutions rather than operate for profit. However, a substantial amount of traffic carried by the Internet is now related to commercial activities in the form of online shopping, banking or entertainment, or to private emails.

The technical aspects of the Internet are controlled by an international group called the Internet Engineering Task Force (IETF - http://www.ietf.org/). Information about the Internet is recorded in documents called RFCs (requests for comments). These documents are available online from several sites, such as the IETF. Some of the RFCs contain official definitions of protocols, but others contain proposals for new protocols or explanatory information about the Internet.

TCP/IP (transmission control protocol/internet protocol) is the name given to a suite of protocols designed for the Internet, but suitable for any internetwork. The Internet contains the following broad classes of network, as shown in sketch below:

- Backbones – providing high-speed data links between networks (e.g. NSFNET, EBONE)
- Regional networks – clusters of networks for specific organizations, such as universities
- Commercial networks – e.g. ISPs (Internet service providers) providing subscribers with access to the Internet or organizations providing their employees with access to the Internet

- National networks – groups of networks covering specific countries
- Local networks – consisting of individual groups of computers such as those on a university campus (e.g. SJSU network)

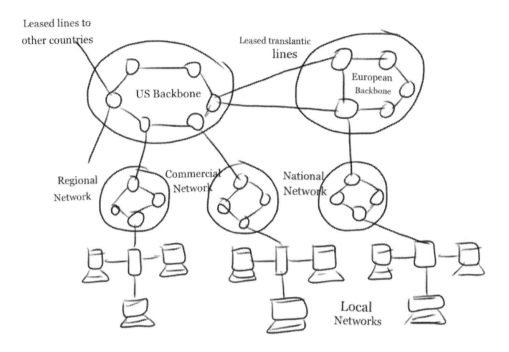

Sketch 5.2   Internet – the network of network

What is Domain Name System?

Applications use easy-to-remember names for hosts on the Internet, but before sending any data to a host an application in the source host must translate its name for the destination host to the numerical network address. The Internet is divided into domains, and an authority in each domain is responsible for allocating names. However, the domains may be divided into sub-domains and the responsibility of allocating sub-domain names may be delegated to other authorities. In this way the names form a tree structure as shown in sketch below. The Internet Assigned Number Authority (IANA) has overall responsibility for assigning domain names on the Internet.

The full names of hosts are written as a sequence of words, separated by full stops, and each word refers to a domain or sub-domain. The names are written from left to right, with the most specific (the host) on the left and the top-level domain on the right. Broadly speaking, there are two classes of domain name – organizational and geographical. You can see from Figure 13 that some organizational names are the same as national names, illustrating the point that the individual domain names are not necessarily unique, but the full host names are. The delegation of naming authority greatly simplifies the allocation of names because the naming authorities in higher domains do not need to be notified about changes to names in the lower domains. However, naming authorities must be able to determine the physical location of hosts in their immediate sub-domain.

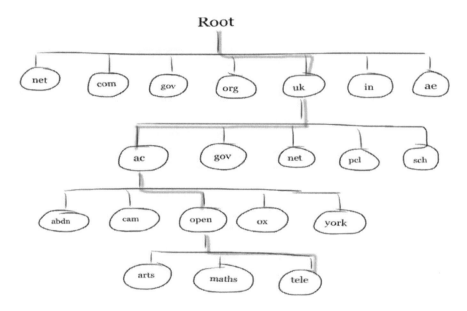

Sketch 5.3   The structure of names on the Internet

The network address determines the path through an internetwork, and the translation from a host name to a network address is typically done by the application invoking a library program called the *resolver*. In principle, the resolver program sends messages to a database that contains the network addresses corresponding to the domain names. It would not be practicable, however, to have a single database for the Internet, so distributed databases, called the **domain name system** (DNS), hold the translation information. Each domain has one or more name servers and, whenever a host has a name to resolve, it sends the host name to a local name server. If the local name server has a record for the name it can reply immediately with the corresponding network address. If not, the local name server passes the query to a name server for a higher-level domain. In the worst case this would be a name server for the top-level domain. The top-level domain name server will at least know the name servers of all its immediate sub-domains, and can supply the local name server with the network address of a name server in the appropriate sub-domain. The local name server then repeats the query to this name server. The process is repeated until the query is satisfied.

What is Hypertext transfer protocol (HTTP)?

The web is an application of the Internet for accessing resources wherever they are located. Each resource on the web is found through a name called a **uniform resource locator** (URL). A URL consists first of the name of the scheme for communicating with the resource at the application layer (e.g. FTP, HTTP, MAILTO) followed by a scheme-specific part. The only scheme we will look at here is HTTP, and the syntax for HTTP URLs takes the form of:

http:// <host> : <port> / <path> ? <search-part>

where 'host' is the domain name as given in the domain name system of the Internet. The 'port' is optional and is described in the next section, but it can be thought of as a way of identifying the different applications that may be running in an application layer. The 'path' in a URL identifies the name of the resource in the host's filing system. The 'search-part' is optional and is used when the resource is a search engine. If no 'port' value is given, then a default value is used.

HTTP takes the form of commands from a client, typically a browser computer program, and responses from a server. A command (called a method in HTTP terminology) can occupy several lines. The first line has the name of the command, the identity of the resource, and the scheme version number. Subsequent lines may contain parameters, which modify the command, and any data to be transferred to the server. Examples of parameters are the name of the host and a date giving the last time a resource was modified. A response from a server takes the form of a status line, additional information about the type of response, and the resource itself. Some example commands are listed in Table 1 and example responses in Table 2.

Table 1: Example HTTP commands

Command Description

Connect	Establishes a tunnel[1] through a proxy server
Delete	Requests the removal of a resource
Get	Requests the retrieval of a resource
Head	Requests the retrieval of information about a resource rather than the resource itself
Options	Requests information about the capabilities of a server or the requirements of a resource
Post	Requests that a resource accepts some information
Put	Requests that a resource is stored at the given location
Trace	Requests that a server takes part in some test

A tunnel is created by encapsulation. A received message is encapsulated in another message so that the received message is transferred transparently through a node or network.

Table 2: Example HTTP responses

Response	Description
100	Continue
200	OK
202	Accepted
302	Found
400	Bad request
404	Not found
406	Not acceptable

Internet Protocol IPv4

IPv4 is the main TCP/IP protocol in the internetwork layer of the TCP/IP reference model. It supports a connectionless service between hosts in an internetwork and its principal function is to forward the protocol data units, called datagrams. This is achieved by each datagram carrying a unique address of its destination. IPv4 addresses may be interpreted in two ways. Initially, they were divided into distinct ranges of addresses called classes, but this proved to be inflexible and now a more flexible scheme, called classless addressing, dominates IPv4 internetworks. The ranges of the four allocated classes of IPv4 addresses are shown in Table 3 below. The values in the table follow the standard dotted-decimal convention of splitting each 32-bit address into four bytes, and expressing the values of the bytes as numbers separated by full stops

Table 3: IPv4 Internet address ranges

Class	Range	
	Lowest	**Highest**
A	0.0.0.0	127.255.255.255
B	128.0.0.0	191.255.255.255
C	192.0.0.0	223.255.255.255
D	224.0.0.0	239.255.255.255

IPv4 address classes A to C identify single hosts, and are called unicast addresses. IPv4 addresses consist of three parts: a prefix identifying the class of address, the address of a network, and the address of a host within the network. For instance, a class C address is identified by the prefix 110, the network address consists of 21 bits, and the host address consists of eight bits. This means that, in principle, there can be $2^{21} = 2097152$ networks in an internetwork with class C addresses, and each single network can have $2^8 = 256$ hosts connected to it. In practice, some addresses are reserved and cannot be allocated to networks or hosts.

Class D addresses are allocated to groups of hosts rather than single hosts. The group is identified by a single 28-bit address, called a multicast address, and the datagram is delivered to all the hosts in the group. Some multicast addresses are reserved for specific groups of hosts, such as all routers connected to a LAN. Other multicast groups can be constructed by hosts sending appropriate management messages. Multicast datagrams are routed through an internetwork by special multicasting routers.

The main benefit of multicasting is that routers can optimize the distribution of datagrams to avoid unnecessary duplication. For instance, if a host wishes to send a single datagram to 100 destinations by unicasting, it has to send 100 copies of the datagram. However, if all the 100 destinations belong to a single multicast group, the originating host can send a single multicast datagram and the routers will duplicate the datagram only where necessary to deliver it to destinations with which they have different interfaces. This reduces the total number of copies of the datagram that exist in the internetwork.

Exercise

1. Identify the components part of the following URL:
   "http://www.bing.com/search?q=hypertext+protocol"
2. Summarize the view, or level of abstraction, each OSI layer provides to its higher layer.
3. Explain the difference between packet switching and circuit switching methods.

Chapter

6

Middleware Software Overview

Chapter Goal

After studying this chapter, you should be able to:

- Learn the role of middleware software in enterprise
- Learn the different middleware software architecture based on RPC, Event and Messages
- Learn how SOA and middleware technology fit together

Introduction to Middleware Software

Today's IT environments are becoming increasingly diverse and complex. As the focus on integration increases, it moves horizontally and extends beyond the boundaries of the individual enterprise to include partners, suppliers, and customers. It is this diversity in IT environments that is increasing the complexity of the challenge that an enterprise has to deal with. That is where middleware comes in.

Middleware is the infrastructure software that simplifies the problem of horizontal integration. The IT infrastructure has to integrate people, data, and applications across and beyond the enterprise to provide benefits throughout the value chain. It is infrastructure middleware that provides the operational resilience that is essential to make the technology transitions that allow an enterprise to react quickly to the necessary business changes and to adapt dynamically in this new business world. The sketch below illustrates the complexity of an IT environment where employees, customers, partners, and vendors need to be connected with each other. Business transactions are generating information that needs to be shared, analyzed and leveraged for competitive advantages. Legacy applications have to be leveraged in service oriented architecture. New applications need to be integrated seamlessly using an enterprise service bus.

The role of modern middleware software is to integrate and simplify. In other words, middleware software provides the foundation for onDemand business. Good news is that most of modern middleware software provides layered architecture where a business can start with small functionality and progressively add function as needed by the business demand. Reference architecture for modern middleware has been discussed in this chapter.

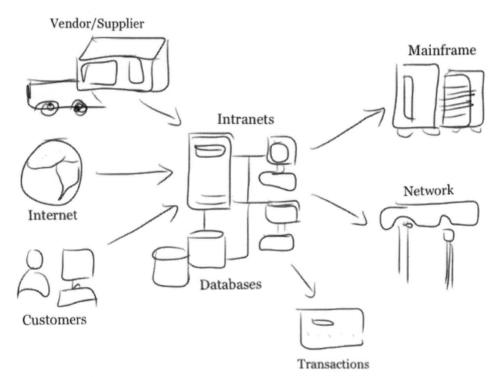

Sketch 6.1 Complexity of typical IT Infrastructure

What are the services provided by Traditional Middleware software?

Middleware comes in different shapes and sizes. Enterprise has choices of choosing commercial solution as well as an open source one. Here are the bare minimum services provided by a traditional middleware. Modern middleware software comes with a lot of bells and whistles and also supports cloud and mobile platform integration. This will be discussed in a later section.

- Facilitates communication mechanism for applications across networks (e.g.. Sending database query results over network)
- Provides platform transparency to the applications.
- Provides network transparency (TCP/IP, NetWare IPX/SPX, and NetBIOS/NetBEUI (Named Pipes)
- Application and Tool Support (ODBC/JDBC)
- Variety of Programming languages support
- Databases support

Why are interfaces so expensive to build and maintain?

There are several reasons: Application interface logic is typically intertwined within application business logic. This is usually due to the nature of the applications themselves. The programming models do not enable the separation of interface logic from the applications themselves. The more tightly integrated the interface, the more difficult the application is to change. The more interfaces within a program, the more complex the application becomes. Over time, and with enough separate connections, the interface logic can, in fact, exceed the business logic. In such circumstances, reuse becomes difficult and impractical. SOA is the methodology and architecture for solving this problem.

What are the services provided by modern Middleware Software?

- Location Transparency; one of the design goals of a distributed system is that the application programmer needs not to be aware of where resources are located.
- Enhanced Security (Encryption of authentication and data)
- Single system login (Directory services like LDAP)
- Database oriented services (Heterogeneous join in a temporary table)
- Applications oriented services (Transaction Processing monitoring, Queuing)
- Management services (Configuration, Performance)

- Interactions with other network services

Layered architecture of a Middleware

- Presentation layer
- Business Processes layer
- Business Services layer
- Data services layer
- Connectivity/Access layer

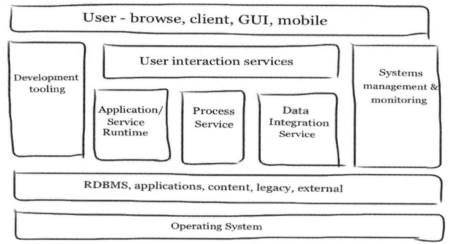

Sketch 6.2   Typical Middleware layered architecture

Application Services Runtime

Runtime services are most important piece of the overall middleware architecture for developers. Often, developers want to adopt and use latest programming techniques in the application development whereas IT operation staff wants to provide a stable operating environment for those applications. This creates a conflict. Developers need agility and choice in their application development frameworks, languages, and programming paradigms. The developer's ideal operating environment requires the flexibility to support

more versions more often. But system administrators want stability and predictability. They don't want developer choices to disrupt operational procedure. Use of latest JVM and JRE to support latest and greatest features can be a good example that could cause potential security problems and create un stability for business users.

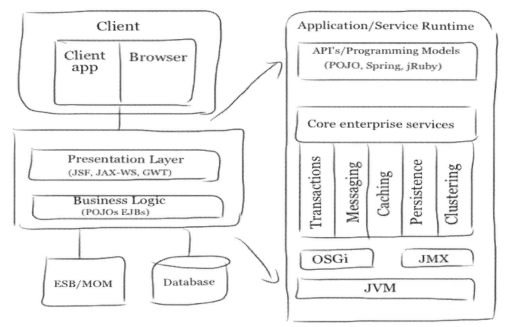

Sketch 6.3   Application Runtime services sub component

The reference architecture provides a core run time services that supports J2EE and OSGi standards (http://www.osgi.org but is flexible enough to support tomorrow's programming models and framework. The main benefit for the enterprise is that one core runtime platform can support all of enterprise's Java applications. It will also be able to support a broad based open source application development framework such as Spring, Google Web Toolkit, Struts or RichFaces. The platform itself can be customized for specific application requirements such as:

- simple servlet deployments
- lightweight java applications
- mission critical applications that require support for clustering, transactions, messaging and web services.

Business Process & Management Services

Enterprise IT is faced with changing business requirements all the time. Mobile app support for existing business processes or moving a traditional client based software application to a new emerging cloud model are some of the great examples todays IT organization faces. These organizations are striving to implement SOA with agility. SOA implementations are often targeted at executing business processes and responding to business events in a faster, more consistent manner. A process orchestration component is therefore typically required. The individual steps of a business process require the execution of business logic, which may include the creation of new business-rule services or the encapsulation of that logic in existing code or web services. The agility that SOA promises requires flexibility—not just in the features of the technology, but also flexibility in the choice of vendor technologies to implement the various components of the SOA stack. Many organizations that have begun to implement SOA have either been forced to build much of it themselves due to the prohibitively high cost of today's commercial SOA offerings or have found themselves implementing inflexible, complex, and expensive SOA software suites.

The reference architecture has brought together a combination of business process management, business rules, service registry, message mediation, and enterprise service bus capabilities. The architecture provides the capabilities and the open standards support that are needed for an enterprise SOA solution, as shown in the right side of the sketch.

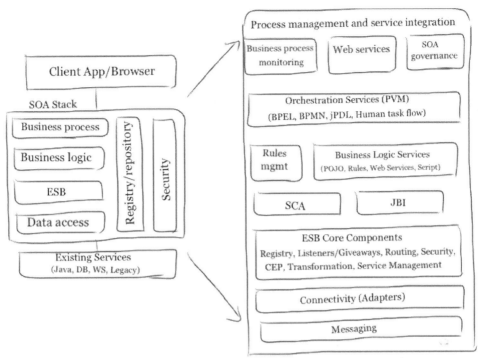

Sketch 6.4 Process service integration architecture overview

Data Integration and Business Intelligence Services

With the emergence of Big data analytics within enterprise, organizations have increasing data volumes, increasing needs for consolidated data views to drive real-time business operations, and increasing drive toward interoperability and standards support. The ability to bridge data gaps in a more straightforward, streamlined, and scalable way is becoming an urgent need. Each of the data integration components identified in the reference architecture above is necessary for a comprehensive approach to data management and data integration. While the ETL style of data integration is used to create a consolidated copy of the source data, data services typically provide data integration and streaming services in real-time without making a copy of the integrated result sets. Data services are key components of a flexible architecture that provides applications with the data views they need while hiding federated data source details and managing data source access.

Today, reality is that organizations need multiple data integration tools and approaches in order to meet various quality, latency, performance, and technology API requirements. In fact, data services capabilities can be combined with an organization's existing BI and ETL investments to accelerate the movement of data architectures toward more service-oriented approaches. The requirement for accelerated access to critical business information has forced organizations to rethink their data integration strategies to accommodate both retrospective analyses and real-time business activity monitoring.

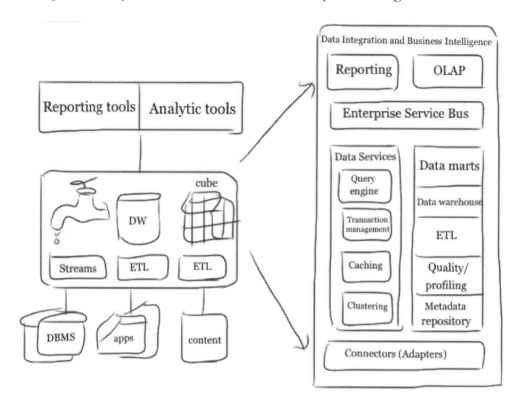

Sketch 6.5 Data Integration services component architecture

User Interaction Services

As organizations continue the drive to become more service-oriented, there's an associated drive toward improving the consumability of applications and services for end users. Business expects that reuse and modularity will occur at all levels, from site-wide to the component level, enabling the delivery of more personalized business applications. The population of power users within organizations will significantly expand as more technically savvy workers enter the workforce. This requires a new generation of user interfaces that allow power users to rapidly configure custom, time-sensitive role based dashboard applications without the need for an IDE or programming skills. In addition, growth in SaaS and cloud computing is driving a mix of on-premise and off-premise systems. All of these trends heighten the demand for portal platforms to provide a highly integrated user experience while promoting the reuse of common site elements, security, UI components, branding, and presentation layer infrastructure. The reference architecture that highlights these user interaction components is shown on the right in the diagram below.

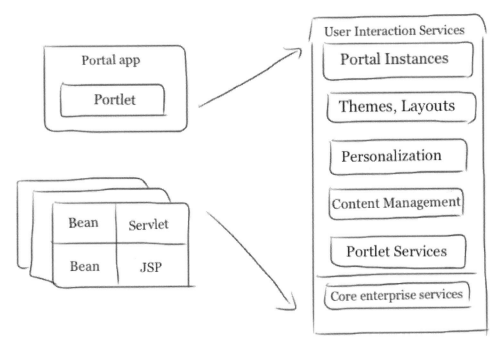

Sketch 6.6 User Interaction services

Development Tooling & System Management Services

Consistent, integrated developer tooling begins with a standard, Eclipse-based development environment that maximizes developer productivity. The use of Eclipse enables extensibility via additional plug-ins as more heterogeneous technologies are required. By integrating the developer tooling with an instance of the runtime platform, middleware software minimizes the version mismatches between development, test, and production environments. This integration, coupled with the lightweight footprint of the runtime platform, provides the benefit of reduced iteration times between development and test efforts. Integrated systems management is required to handle the administration and maintenance challenges found in typical datacenters, where applications are deployed across development, QA, staging, and production. The results of these challenges are applications that have multiple versions and potentially inconsistent configurations, access privileges, and release cycles. The architecture of the integrated management solution helps to solve these challenges by including a centralized management server and auto-discovery agents for the inventory of distributed resources. Organizations with complex environments benefit from administration features that include the start/stop deployment of services and applications, patch management, monitoring, and alerts. Because the reference architecture spans multiple technologies, the types of resources that are monitored range from low-level OS statistics and detailed application processes (e.g., EJBs, URL response times) to business processes, message queues, and data access requests. Data center operators' benefit from this improved manageability and visibility, which provides more consistency and efficiency in managing application systems and results in lower cost of ownership. Organizations also benefit from the governance of system artifacts and security policies, ensuring that critical system information is stored, versioned, and audited, as well as retrievable by development, operations, and management teams.

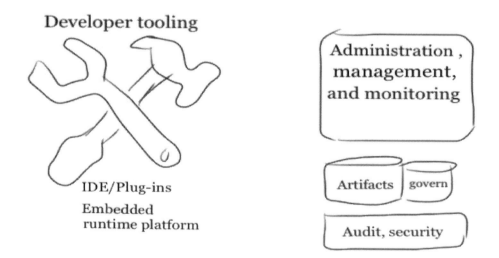

Developer tooling

IDE/Plug-ins
Embedded
runtime platform

Administration ,
management,
and monitoring

Artifacts | govern

Audit, security

Sketch 6.7   Developer tooling and System Management Services architecture

Types of Middleware

1. Remote Procedure Call (RPC) based middleware

RPC allows procedures in one application to call procedures in remote applications as if they were local calls. Developers define functions using an interface description language (IDL), and then compile that function into client and server stubs that actually do the networking. So, to call these functions, the developer uses function calls within a development tool The key for the developer is whether the RPC-based middleware generates functions in the tool actually used to develop applications in. While many 4GL tools can call C functions, it is easier if the functions show up more natively. One might say that developers create their own APIs using RPC-based solutions. For applications that have been multiuser system based but are now being distributed, the RPC approach is very intuitive: Each existing function can be split across the network as needed.

The middleware implements a linking mechanism that locates remote procedures and makes these transparently available to a caller. Traditionally, this type of middleware handled procedure-based programs; it now also includes object-based components.

2. Object Request Broker or ORB-based middleware

ORB based middleware enables an application's objects to be distributed and shared across heterogeneous networks. An ORB just lets the developer of an application composed of many objects easily partition those objects onto different network nodes. It's like the RPC-based approach, except this time it's for object-oriented tools and not function-oriented tools. If the object-oriented developer does not get an ORB, the programming job will be complicated by having to create links between objects and the functions or other APIs offered by the other middleware solutions. That's more work. The ORB world has many standards, most generically the Object Management Group's Common Object Request Broker Architecture (CORBA) but also including defacto standards like Microsoft's OLE

3. Message Oriented Middleware or MOM-based middleware
Allows distributed applications to communicate and exchange data by sending and receiving messages. MOM is the focus of this chapter.

4. Event based Middleware

Event based middleware capture changes in event(a car gets sold at dealership), which is consumed by various applications within the architecture to take appropriate actions.

Message Oriented Middleware (MOM)

MOM offers a very basic set of commands with which to communicate over the network, often as few as SEND and RECEIVE. Application developers then create application-specific functions or routines built on top of these basic functions. As far as transports go, the interface itself is even simpler than programming to a particular network transport API like TCP/IP sockets, and the message-oriented API is provided for whatever network transports are actually supported by the vendor, not just for one single protocol.

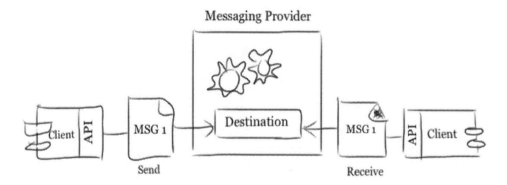

Sketch 6.8 Message oriented middleware architecture

Here are the key things to learn about MOM:

1. Messaging is an asynchronous method of passing information between programs.
2. Queuing is a method of passing information indirectly through message queues. Messages are stored in queues until the recipient is ready to read it.
3. Online messaging is in real time, with message delivery typically occurring in seconds or even sub-seconds. MOM products guarantee delivery of high-value messages.
4. Applications are isolated from communication network, which make applications simpler, shields them from network changes, and provides greater network independence.

5. Queue based processing makes it easy to transparently add servers as the workload increases, providing better load balancing.
6. Message queues can be read as FIFO or priority basis. Queues can be read at the same time they are updated that reduces the concept of batch window time.

It is not uncommon to find a system, which uses both RPC and MOM technology to solve business problem. Think about an airline reservation system, in which a consolidation system like Expedia (used just as an example) implements RPC based system to manage user id and preferences information and a Message based system to connect to all airline operator's systems that subscribe to its services. Again on other side, individual airline operator such as United or Delta may have an RPC based system implemented.

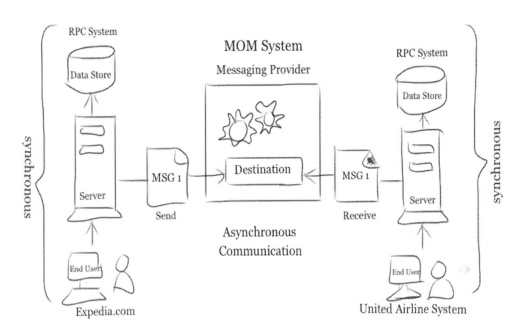

Sketch 6.9 A RPC and MOM combined middleware architecture

Message Queue Overview

A message queue is a programming object, which facilitates program to program communication.

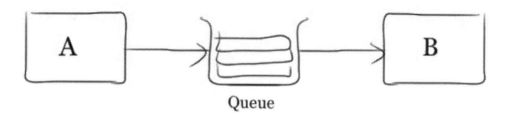

Sketch 6.10 Program to program communication using a message queue

The sketch above depicts the basic mechanism by which this communication takes place. Program A prepares a message and puts it on a queue. Program B then gets the message from a queue and processes it. Both Program A and Program B use an application programming interface (API) to put messages on a queue and get messages from a queue. Note that when Program A puts a message on the queue, Program B may not be executing. The queue stores the message safely until Program B starts and is ready to get the message. Likewise, at the time when Program B gets the message from the queue, Program A may no longer be executing. A message queue offers some of great features for a transaction system:

- Integrate virtually everything
- Assured delivery: A message will always be delivered if used with proper options
- Enabling remote devices (sensors, RFIDs, smart meters)
- Backbone of ESB (future growth and integration)
- Reliable file transfer
- Integrated support for web services
- Standard programming interface(MQI) on all supported platforms
- Supports clustering for dynamically distributed messaging workload
- Time-independent processing
- Supports advance message security

Synchronous Application Design

The sketch below shows how Program B can send a message to Program A using the same mechanism. The message may be a reply to a message it received from Program A. Typically, Program B uses a different queue to send messages to Program A. Using a separate queue is not strictly necessary, but doing so leads to a simpler application design and simpler programming logic. If Program A sends a message to Program B and expects a reply, one option is for Program A to put a message on Queue 1 and then wait for the reply to appear on Queue 2. This is called the synchronous model for two-way communication between programs. Using the synchronous model, Program A and Program B would normally be executing at the same time. However, if Program B fails, Program A might potentially have to wait a long time for a reply. How long Program A should wait before continuing with other processing is a design issue.

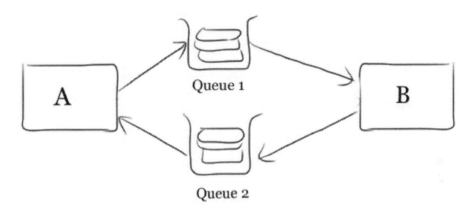

Sketch 6.11 Program to program communication using synchronous design

Asynchronous Application Design

In asynchronous application design, program A puts messages on Queue 1 for Program B to process, but it is Program C, acting asynchronously to Program A, which receives replies from Queue 2 and processes them. Typically, Program A and Program C would be part of the same application. The asynchronous model is a natural model for most modern MQ based implementation. Program A can continue to put messages on Queue 1 and is not blocked by having to wait for a reply to each message. It can continue to put messages on Queue 1 even if Program B fails. In that case, Queue 1 stores the messages safely until Program B is restarted. In a variation of the asynchronous model, Program A could put a sequence of messages on Queue 1, optionally continue with other processing, and then return to get and process the replies from Queue 2 itself.

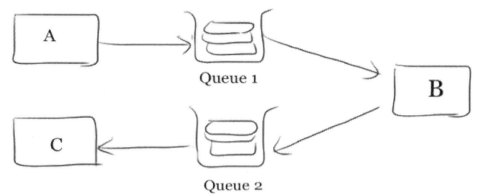

Queue 1

Queue 2

Sketch 6.12 Program to program communication using Asynchronous design

Time Independence

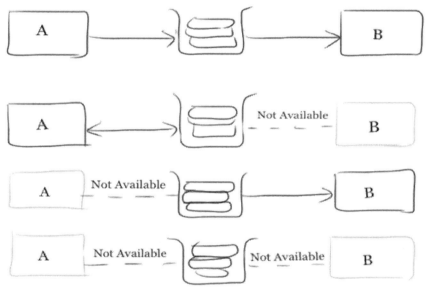

Sketch 6.13 Time Independence in MQ architecture

This figure demonstrates that Program A puts messages on the queue and Program B gets them when it is ready. If Program B is busy or is not available, the messages are stored safely in the queue until it is ready to get them. If, at the point when B becomes ready, Program A has completed it's processing or has failed, it does not matter. Program B can still get the messages and process them. Indeed, there may be times when neither program is available, but any outstanding messages are still stored safely in the queue.

Styles of Communication

Conversational or transaction-oriented communication is characterized by two or more programs executing simultaneously in a cooperative manner in order to perform a transaction. They communicate with each other through an architected interface. While one program is waiting for a reply from another program with which it is cooperating, it may continue with other processing. APPC, CPI-C, and the sockets interface to TCP/IP are examples of this style of communication.

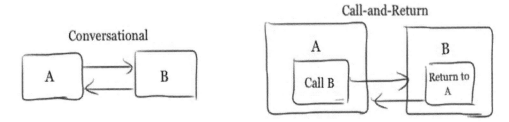

Sketch 6.14 Communication styles

The call-and-return style is similar, but when one program calls another program, the first program is blocked and cannot perform any other processing until the second program returns control to it. Remote procedure call (RPC) is an example of this style of communication.

In the messaging style, communicating programs can execute independently of each other. An executing program receives input in the form of messages and also outputs its results as messages. A message that is the output from one program becomes the input to another program, but there is no requirement that the latter must be executing when the former outputs the message. Contrast this with the conversational and call-and-return styles where all cooperating partners must be executing at the same time. IBM WebSphere MQ uses this messaging style.

Messaging

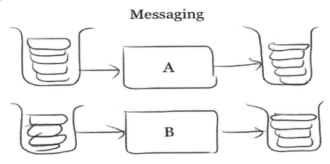

Sketch 6.15 Communication styles (Messaging)

Local & Remote Queues

When an application opens a queue, the queue manager determines whether the ultimate destination queue is owned by the queue manager to which the application is connected (a *local* queue), or whether it is one owned by another queue manager (a *remote* queue).

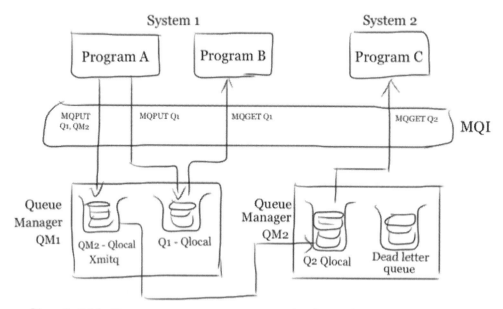

Sketch 6.16 Program to program communication using remote queues

When the application subsequently puts a message on a queue that is local, the queue manager places the message directly on that queue. However, if the queue is remote, the queue manager places the message instead on a special local queue called a transmission queue. It is then the task of message channel agents, to get the message from the transmission queue and send it over the network to a message channel agent at the receiving end. The receiving MCA then puts the message on the destination queue. Once the message has been safely committed on the destination queue, it is removed from the transmission queue. If the receiving MCA cannot put the message on the destination queue for any reason, the message either will be placed in the dead letter queue associated with that queue manager, or the message will be discarded, depending on the options specified by the sending application in the message descriptor.

A Message

A message is generally composed of two parts: a header and data. All messages will always have a header called the MQ *message descriptor* (MQMD). The message descriptor contains control information about the message that is used by both the queue manager and the receiving application. The application data is meaningful only to the applications that send or receive the message. It is possible to have a message with only a header and no application data.

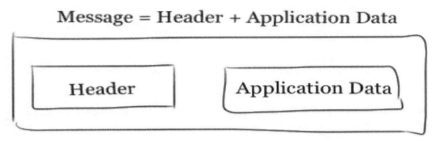

Sketch 6.17   A MQ message

Application Design using MQ

Parallel Design

This model allows several requests to be sent by an application without the application having to wait for a reply to one request before sending the next. All the requests can then be processed in parallel. Designing the system in this way can improve the overall response time. To book a vacation with a travel agent may require a number of tasks. In the scenario depicted in the figure, an agent needs to reserve a flight and a hotel room, and rent a car. All of these tasks must be performed before the overall business transaction can be considered complete. Using MQ, a request message can be put on each of three queues, which serve the car rental application, the flight reservations application, and the hotel reservations application. Each application can perform its respective task in parallel with the other two and then put a reply message on the reply-to queue. The agent's application can then get the three replies and produce a consolidated answer. This model allows several requests to be sent by an application without the application having to wait for a reply to one request before sending the next. All the requests can then be processed in parallel. Designing the system in this way can improve the overall response time.

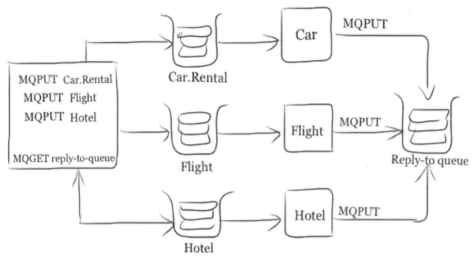

Sketch 6.18 A travel reservation application design using MQ

Application Design – Client Server

The message descriptor of each request message plays an important role here. One of the fields in the message descriptor is the name of the reply-to queue. This informs the server application where to put the reply message. In this way, each client application can receive its replies separately from those of the other client applications.

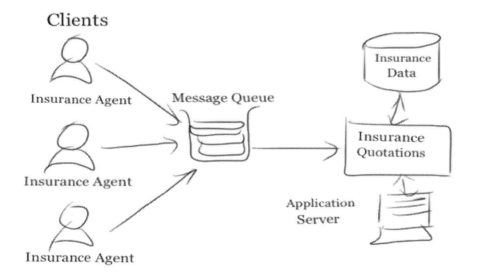

Sketch 6.19 A client server based application design using MQ

The server application (insurance quotations) can handle requests from multiple client applications. Each application client is identical, and requests information from the application server. The message descriptor in each of the incoming messages identifies the appropriate reply-to queue for each request, so that the application server knows where to route the reply message to.

Java Messaging Service (JMS)

Java Message Service (JMS) is a set of interfaces and associated semantics that define how a JMS client accesses the facilities of an enterprise messaging product. It provides a common way for Java programs to create, send, receive, and read messages to and from an enterprise messaging system. The JMS API is a standard developed by Sun, IBM, and other enterprise solution vendors. IBM Web Sphere MQ is an example of JMS provider that implements JMS for a messaging product.

When should you use JMS API?

An enterprise application provider is likely to choose a messaging API like JMS over a tightly coupled API, such as Remote Procedure Call (RPC), under the following circumstances:

- The provider wants the components not to depend on information about other components' interfaces, so that components can be easily replaced.
- The provider wants the application to run whether or not all components are up and running simultaneously.
- The application business model allows a component to send information to another and to continue to operate without receiving an immediate response.

For example, components of an enterprise application for an retailer can use the JMS API in situations like these:

- The retailer component can send a message to the vendor component when the inventory level for a product goes below a certain level, so the vendor can fulfill the order for the product.

- The vendor component can send a message to the shipping components so that the shipping company picks up the products for shipping.
- The shipping components in turn can send messages to the retailer and vendor with scheduled arrival and update their information.

Open Message Queue (OpenMQ)

OpenMQ is a full featured Message Oriented Middleware (MOM) server, which implements JMS API. OpenMQ consists of the following components:

Message broker or messaging server

Message broker is the heart of the messaging system. It manages the message queues, manages the client connections and their requests, control the client access to the queues for reading /writing.

Client libraries

Client libraries provide APIs, which enable developers to interact with the message broker from different programming languages. OpenMQ provides Java and C libraries in addition to a platform and programming language agnostic interfaces.

Administration tools

Admin tools interface provide easy to use tools for message broker life cycle management, broker monitoring and message destination life cycle management. The sketch below illustrates the various components of OpenMQ:

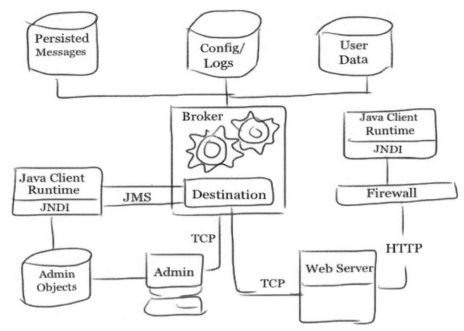

Sketch 6.20 OpenMQ component overview

Enterprise Service Bus

An enterprise service bus (ESB) includes the necessary capabilities of a high-performance, reliable messaging infrastructure that provides protocol gateways and adapters with embedded routing and transformation. But it also extends beyond these core capabilities by bundling process management, human workflow, business rules, security, governance, and service registry functions with the ESB. This combined functionality seamlessly blends logic from web applications, legacy systems, and databases in new SOA-based applications. It then extends those services with new logic for business process orchestration, business rules, and event-driven message correlation.

What are the main services provided by ESB?

SOA solves the problem created by Enterprise Application Integration. ESB provides platform for SOA implementation. In essence ESB provides:

- JMS implementation to return data as a response to service consumer requests over http
- Security
- Service level agreement

- Routing
- Transformation

Apache Open Source Middleware products

- Reliable messaging with <u>Apache ActiveMQ</u>
- Messaging, routing and Enterprise Integration Patterns with <u>Apache Camel</u>
- WS-* and RESTful web services with <u>Apache CXF</u>
- Loosely coupled integration between all the other components with Apache ServiceMix NMR including rich Event, Messaging and Audit API
- Complete WS-BPEL engine with <u>Apache ODE</u> (Orchestration Director Engine)
- OSGi-based server runtime powered by <u>Apache Karaf</u>

Complex Event Processing (CEP)

CEP is an approach that identifies data and application traffic as "events" of importance, correlates these events to reveal predefined patterns, and reacts to them by generating "actions" to systems, people and devices. CEP provides a system, which facilitates an action triggered not by a **single event**, but by a **complex composition of events, happening at different times, and within different contexts. Fraud detection** in an online financial transaction in real time is a good example. A combination of events such as logging in, changing password and transferring money to a different account can trigger an alert to the system that calls the owner of the account for verification of that transaction or simply denying the transaction. In summary, CEP is all about getting better information in **real time**.

A CEP system consists of the following components:

1. CEP Rule Engine: detects conditions based on a combination of events.
2. CEP Authoring Tool: Event processing language (EPL) such as Oracle™ EPL is used in an integrated development environment to define business rules. These tools help define complex and intricate rules easily.
3. In modern middleware software such as IBM Websphere, CEP is part of the ESB architecture that provides event services.

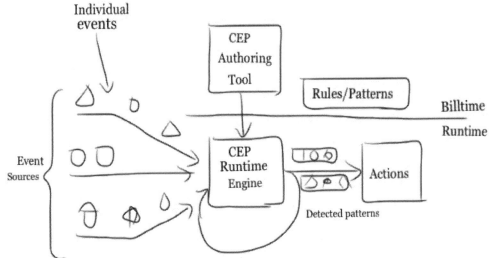

Sketch 6.21 A complex event processing system overview

Some typical examples of CEP applications are:

- Event driven rules in Insurance underwriting process
- Finance (algorithmic trading, fraud detection, risk management)
- Network and application monitoring (intrusion detection, SLA monitoring)
- Sensor network applications (RFID reading, scheduling and control of fabrication lines, air traffic)

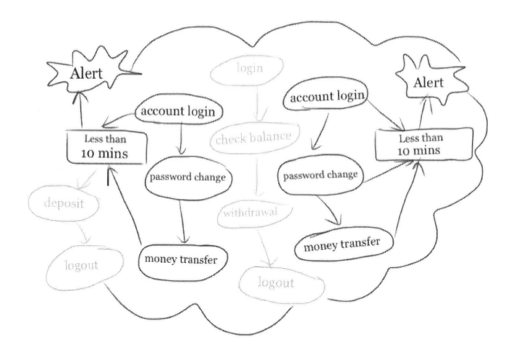

Sketch 6.22 CEP – Fraud detection model

Event Based Middleware for Java and Scala – Akka

Akka is a toolkit and runtime for building highly concurrent, distributed, and fault tolerant event-driven applications on the JVM. Akka aims to solve the complexity of writing concurrent and scalable and highly available applications and supported on both Scala and Java programming language. Akka's architecture is based on:

- Actor concurrency model
- Software transactional memory
- Asynchronous message passing

Exercise

1. Study the potential use cases of CEP as given below:

- **Regulatory constraints:** Report on a bulk buys transaction that is performed less than one day after a bulk sell.
- **Fraud detection:** Report when two credit card purchases are performed within an hour at a distance greater than 300 miles.
- **Aggregation:** Report at a set time (e.g. the end of a business day) the number of purchase requests that were processed, their total dollar amount and the average dollar amount.
- **Customer Relationship Management:**
- Alert if three orders from the same platinum customer were rejected for the same reason during a 24-hour period
- Alert if an order was sent for processing and no response was received within the time specified by the SLA
- **Intelligent Routing:** Route a trade message through SWIFT (Global provider of secure financial messages). If acknowledge is not received within 10 minutes and the trade $ value is higher than threshold try again. If acknowledge is not received after 3 attempts use telex (Intercom system).
- Come up on a report with challenges, solution and benefits for these use cases.

2. **Create a simple application using Event based middleware Akka**
   - Download Typesafe Activator from (http://typesafe.com/platform/getstarted)
   - Follow the instructions to start Typesafe Activator UI
   - Create a sample application

Chapter

7

Distributed Systems

Chapter Goal

After studying this chapter, you should be able to:
- Learn and describe some of the architectural and programming paradigms used in distributed system development
- Describe message passing and the role of protocols within a message passing paradigm
- Describe how event-based architectures are used within distributed system development
- Introduce one implementation of an event-based architecture

Distributed models

Before looking in detail at some of the technologies it is worth examining some of the implementation and design models that can be used for distributed system development .ranging from the familiar, message passing, to the unfamiliar, tuple-based technology.

While studying distributed models, we will first describe the variety of methods and architectures that are available and the degree of closeness they have to Internet technologies such as TCP/IP, for example message passing is close in concept to the idea of data flowing down a transmission line, while tuple-based development views a distributed system as just a big, persistent store of objects. The distributed models that we will look at in this chapter are: message passing, distributed objects, remote procedure call, event-based technology and tuple-based technology.

Message passing Architecture

Message passing is the simplest form of development paradigm. For example, the way that a client running a browser communicates with a web server is via message passing. Take an example of Chrome extensions, an RSS reader extension might use content script to detect the presence of an RSS feed on a webpage, then notify the background page in order to display a page action icon for that page. Such communications between extensions and their content script works using message passing. Either side can listen for messages sent by the other end. A message can contain a JSON object.

Message passing is based on the idea of a protocol; a language that embodies the functions required by one entity in a distributed system (usually a client), which another entity provides (usually a server). As an example of a protocol consider Table 1. It shows the protocol associated with a naming service. This is a service in a distributed system, which associates a name with some resource in the system. For example, it might associate the location of a file within the distributed system with some symbolic name.

Table 1: An example of a simple protocol for a client of a naming service

Function	Meaning
Find *Name*	Finds the resource identified by *Name*
Delete *Name*	Deletes the resource identified by *Name*
Add *Name, Resource*	Adds a new resource identified by *Name*
Modify *Name, Resource*	Changes the resource identified by *Name*

Table 2: An example of a simple protocol for a server that implements a naming service

Function	Meaning
DeleteOK	Deletion of a resource has been carried out successfully
AddOK	Addition of a resource has been carried out successfully
ModifyOK	Modification of a resource has been carried out successfully
Error *Errorcode*	An error has occurred, the nature of the error can be found within the error code value
Resource *Resourcedetails*	A find has been carried out successfully and the resource returned by the client and associated with the name provided

Effectively a naming service provides a lookup service for a distributed system. A client using the naming service detailed in Table 1 would communicate with the server implementing the naming service using sockets. It would send messages such as

Delete Employee "John Doe"

to delete a name/resource pair identified by the string *"John Doe"* and to find details of the resource(s) identified by the string *"John Doe"*.

Find "John Doe"

Table 1 shows only one half of a protocol: that associated with client messages; most protocols will also contain the messages sent by a server. For example, Table 2 shows a selection of messages, which could be sent by the server implementing the name service.

If a client asked for a resource associated with a name using a Find message and that resource was successfully identified by the server implementing the name service, then the server would return with the string Resource Details where Details was the details of the resource associated with the name provided by the Find message that was issued.

The best known naming service is the **domain naming system** in the Internet, which associates domain names with IP addresses. However, many distributed systems contain their own naming service for resources such as files and collections of data. Such a service provides a simple way of insulating a distributed system from changes in physical details, for example when a file is moved from one computer to another. For example, a naming service might provide lookup for the symbolic names of files, which are stored at a server in a distributed system. Every program, which accessed files, would consult the naming service before carrying out any processing. If a file location changed then all that would change would be the data held by the naming service, the programs, which accessed the files, would not need to be changed.

Naming and directory services

A directory service is a type of very flexible, naming service, which contains data about the resources and users of a distributed system. For example, if you want to write a program, which discovers what the fastest printer is in a distributed system, then the program will consult a directory service. Almost certainly one of the most popular directory services is LDAP (Lightweight Directory Access Protocol). Its roots lie in the development of the OSI Reference Model when a standard called X500 was developed as a part of the OSI effort. Unfortunately X500 was far too complicated and heavy in terms of facilities, even for large distributed systems, and a number of much lighter directory services have emerged over the last decade and become popular. These include LDAP, Novell Directory Services (NDS), Sun's Network Information Services (NIS and NIS+) and the Windows NT Domains from Microsoft. Java has a standard API known as JNDI (Java Naming and Directory Interface), which is able to interface with all these directory services.

Fixed and adaptive protocols

The protocol described above for a simple naming service is an example of a **fixed protocol**. This is a protocol whose vocabulary is fixed: it is embedded in the client and server's code and data and does not change. An adaptive protocol is one where the protocol changes. A fixed protocol could change over a period of time because the functionality provided by a server changes. However, this change will be over months or years rather than over seconds.

There are some instances where a strictly fixed protocol is not adequate. The most common reason for this is where an application supports variable numbers of arguments. For example, a protocol for a server, which supports the functions of reporting on system usage, might consist of a command, which asks for the identities of the current users of the system. The reply to this service request might consist of anything from zero to thousands of user identities. Another example is where the types of the entities in a protocol command might vary, for example a banking application might require the balance of an account to be returned for either the name of an account holder or the unique integer key which identifies the account.

Another example where an adaptive protocol might be used is when a client and a server have to negotiate some subset of a protocol, which they both understand: for example, the client may only understand an early subset of a protocol while the server understands the full up-to-date version of the protocol. This type of negotiation occurs in client-server systems, which form part of multimedia applications.

A further example of a need to make protocols adaptive is where a highly reliable service is required and where circumstances such as functional changes necessitate a protocol being modified without a server being taken out of service for a significant time or, ideally, not taken out of service at all.

There are a number of techniques used for implementing adaptable protocols; these range from simple ones such as adding extra arguments to a protocol command to indicate the number of arguments that have been provided or an argument which identifies the type of the argument, to the use of serializable objects which embed the functionality of a command within the protocol.

Serializable objects

Serialization is the process whereby objects are turned into raw data so that they can be sent over a transmission medium. Many Java distributed technologies such as the RMI distributed object technology need to send such objects over a network and hence they need to be able to be converted into their raw data. In Java this is done very simply by specifying that a class implements the Serializable interface.

Synchronous and asynchronous message passing

Synchronous message passing involves one entity (usually a client) in the message passing process sending a message and a second entity (usually a server) receiving it, carrying out some processing and then sending back some response which the first entity processes in some way. While the second entity is carrying out the processing the first entity pauses, waiting for the response. In asynchronous message passing each entity in the process does not have to wait for the next part of the dialogue they are engaged in and can carry out some other task. For example, the server could be carrying out some processor-intensive task for another service that it provides. This form of message passing, where there is no close coordination between message passing entities, is known as **asynchronous message passing**.

One way of implementing this would be to place protocol messages on some intermediate queue middleware that would be periodically interrogated by a client; in between interrogating the middleware the client would carry out useful work. This is the idea behind message-oriented middleware.

Benefits of Message passing architecture

Shared memory systems may be easier to program, but are difficult to scale up to a large number of processors. If scalability to larger systems was to continue, systems had to use message passing techniques. It is apparent that message passing systems are the only way to efficiently increase the number of processors managed by a multiprocessor system.

Distributed objects technology

This technology virtually hides the network from the designer and programmer. A distributed object is an object which is resident on one computer and for which methods can be invoked associated with code resident on other computers. A good distributed objects technology should totally hide the underlying communication details from the programmer, for example when a programmer wants to invoke the method *updateRate()* on an object called Mortgage, then the programmer should write the code *Mortgage.updateRate()* in the same form as if the object was contained in the computer in which the code is resident. There should be no references to ports, sockets and server sockets.

The vast majority of distributed objects schemes involve the generation of 'under the cover' code, which carries out the actual processes of sending messages to objects and transmitting the data associated with such messages. Two distributed objects technologies are CORBA, which is a multi-language technology, and RMI, which is a Java-based technology.

Distributed objects technology works by intercepting calls to distributed objects and executing system code which carries out the process of locating objects and sending data and execution instructions. All this is carried out 'under the cover' with the programmer not being forced to include communication code. The architecture of a distributed objects system is shown in sketch below. Here, a number of objects spread around a collection of computers communicate by invoking methods, all data transfer being carried out by means of arguments to the method calls that correspond to the messages.

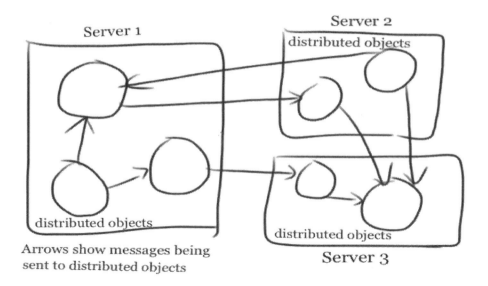

Server 1

Server 2
distributed objects

distributed objects

Arrows show messages being
sent to distributed objects

distributed objects
Server 3

Sketch 7.1 A distributed object bus architecture

Event Driven Bus architecture

The idea of event based bus is similar to the event processing in Graphical user interfaces. Developing such an interface consists of a number of steps:

- A visual object such as a button is placed in a container such as an applet or a frame object.
- An object such as a container implements a listener interface.
- Methods in the interface that the container implements will react to events such as a button being clicked or a pull-down menu being activated and an item selected. The code for these methods is provided within the container class.
- Finally, code is placed either in the constructor for the container or in the init method for an applet, which registers the container as a listener to certain events such as a button being clicked.

This model of processing is based on code being written which responds to events such as a button being clicked, a window being closed and text being deleted from a text box. The same model of processing is used in bus architectures. An example of such an architecture is shown in sketch 3 below. Here a bus connects a number of listener objects to a transmitter object that sends data along the bus. When data appears on the bus each listener object is executed to read and process the data.

In order to listen to data, which is being transferred across a bus the listener objects have to be, registered with the bus in the same way that event handlers need to be registered when developing visual interfaces.

An object bus is very much like a radio transmitter in that listeners to a radio station tune into a channel and receive data (sound) transmitted by the radio transmitter. In the bus architecture listener objects tune into a channel (subscribe) and receive objects that are dispatched along the bus.

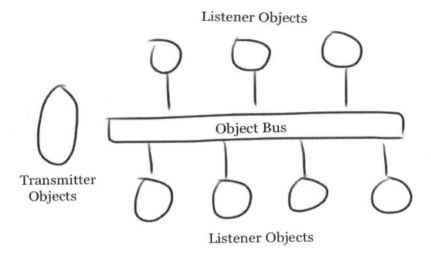

Sketch 7.2   Event driven bus architecture

The model here is somewhat different to that of the distributed object model. In that model, objects communicate with other objects via method calls; invariably the client initiates the processing with the server being a passive entity until it receives some request for a service. This is an example of **pull technology** where clients *pull* data from servers. The object bus model is an example of **push technology** where the server is *pushing* data out to the clients which, when they receive it, carry out some processing action.

The object bus architecture is particularly well suited to applications where real time events are being generated and have to be processed by a dynamically changing collection of listener objects. Typical applications include:

- The delivery of stock market data to financial subscribers on a real-time basis.

- Teleconferencing applications where messages from conference participants have to be broadcast in real-time to other participants.
- Distributed multimedia applications such as video on demand where large chunks of data have to be delivered to subscribers on a real-time basis.
- Conversational applications such as chat rooms where a number of participants communicate with each other in real-time.

Hub and spoke architectures

There are two main types of bus architectures. These are **hub and spoke architectures** and **multicast bus architectures**. Figure 4 shows a typical hub and spoke architecture.

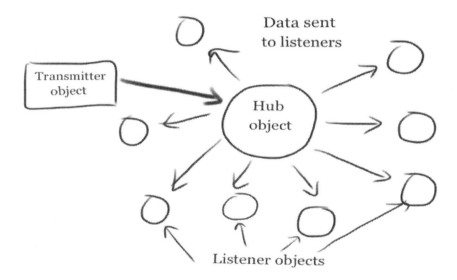

Sketch 7.3 A hub and spoke architecture

It consists of a central hub object that carries out the transmission of data to listener objects. Each listener responds to the event of objects being dispatched to the hub object from a transmitter object that produces the objects to be broadcast. In such architecture there might be one hub object per channel or a single master object serving all the channels. This type of architecture is one of the easiest to implement since it can be developed using base technologies such as RMI or socket and server socket objects. It also has the advantage that since all objects pass through the hub object, accounting and management functions can be centralized on this object. The main disadvantage of this approach, as compared with the multicast bus architecture approach, is that it can generate large amounts of traffic. There is also a reliability problem in that when the server containing the hub malfunctions the whole system goes down.

Multicast bus architectures

This form of technology, like the hub and spoke approach, allows the broadcasting of messages to a number of receivers. Some of the implementations of bus architectures are rooted in multicasting, a technique that allows data to be broadcast to a number of clients. However, some, like the industrial example *iBus* detailed later in this unit, are a sort of software implementation of an Ethernet, where objects are sent down a bus and only processed by any receiver that requires the object; if it isn't required it is passed on to the next receiver.

Multicasting can be thought of as a primitive form of broadcasting of packets. It is carried out using Unreliable Datagram packets (UDP) that are broadcast out on a multicast IP address. Because it is based on UDP, multicasting will suffer from loss of packets when a network is congested. In Java multicasting is based on the java.net.MulticastSocketclass, which is an extension of the Datagram Socket class.

Tuple architecture

So far we saw approaches to build distributed applications such as message passing and Java RMI. The another radical approach to developing distributed systems is based on a coordination language technology called Linda developed by Dr. David Gelerntner at Yale University The language, and its associated technology, has always been thought of highly by other academicians within the distributed systems area, but has never taken off in terms of commercial use. However, in the late 1990s Sun developed a version of the Linda technology as part of its JINI (now knows as Apache River). The main goal of gini was to create the interfacing of disparate technologies into a distributed system: JINI envisages hardware such as burglar alarms, coffee machines, refrigerators, video recorders and mobile phones being seamlessly integrated into distributed systems using uniform interfaces.

The part of JINI, which has been inspired by Linda, is known as *JavaSpaces*. It views a distributed system as consisting of one or more spaces each of which contains objects that can be read from or written to. This is shown in the sketch below:

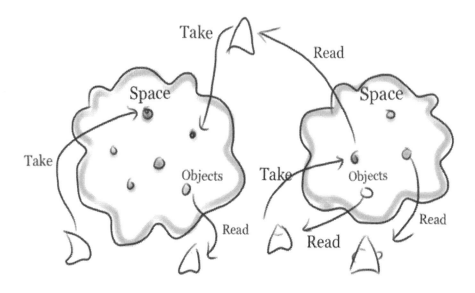

Sketch 7.4   The JavaSpaces architecture

A distributed system can consist of a number of spaces that do not have to be allocated individually to each computer on a network: the spaces could be shared by a number of computers. In sketch above the distributed system is split up into three areas; each of these is known as a **space**. A space is a persistent object store in which objects exist; theoretically they can exist forever. Clients can access these spaces using three operations. They are:

- *Write*. Clients can write new objects to a space.
- *Read*. Clients can read an object's contents from a space.
- *Take*. Clients can read an object from a space and remove it completely from the space.

There are a number of important points to make about JavaSpaces technology.

- Data can be held in a space permanently; in effect this makes JavaSpaces a rudimentary implementation of a distributed persistent object store.

- Spaces are shared: client objects can access the same space concurrently. Concurrent access to shared objects brings with it a number of advantages, but also some rather tricky programming problems. A major advantage *of* JavaSpaces technology is that many of these programming problems are hidden under the bonnet and the programmer does not have to worry about them.

- Objects stored in a space are associative. This means that they are retrieved using some unique attribute or sets of attributes. For example, if the objects were credit cards then they would be retrieved using the unique credit card number associated with each card. Programming using JavaSpaces involves using associative lookup, where a key is used to read, take or write to an object stored in a space. The effect of this is that the JavaSpaces API is very simple consisting of a very small number of methods.

- Spaces are transitionally secure. For example, a transaction in a retail e-commerce system might consist of changes to a sales database, stock database and a credit card transaction database. The key idea about a transaction is that it either succeeds, or totally fails in that none of its operations will succeed if a problem occurs during its execution. When a technology enforces this property then it is known as **transitionally secure**. The implication here is that the programmer does not have to write complicated code to ensure this property every time a transaction is executed. In *JavaSpaces* transactions are supported on a single space or over a number of spaces.

The main disadvantage of a tuple-space-based approach is that it is somewhat inefficient compared, for example, with a message passing architecture. In gaining conceptual simplicity it has lost performance.

Parallel vs. Distributed computing

Parallel computing refers to multiple CPUs performing jobs within the same shared memory system. The main challenge is splitting the work into unit of work i.e. partitioning. Distributed computing refers to multiple computers with their own memory communicating and accomplishing intensive work.

Problems with Parallel Computing

Parallel computing comes with its own challenges, notable the following:

- How do we assign work units to worker threads?
- What if we have more work units than threads?
- How do we aggregate the results at the end?
- How do we know all the workers have finished?
- What if the work cannot be divided into completely separate tasks?

Thread Level Parallelism

Thread level parallelism refers to splitting a program into independent tasks so the work can be accomplished by multiple threads of a process concurrently. The example is a parallel summation task. In the sketch below in the left half, a single thread is executing all 4 tasks in a serial manner hence total execution time for all 4 task is the sum of execution times taken to execute individual tasks. On the other hand in right side of the sketch, 4 tasks have been picked up by 4 threads in parallel and they run these tasks on 4 different CPU cores on a system. In this case, total execution time will be maximum time taken by an individual task.

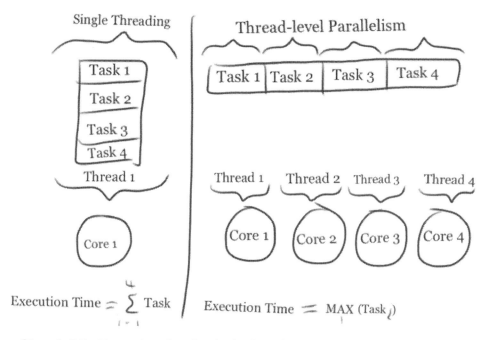

Execution Time $= \sum_{i=1}^{4} Task$ Execution Time $=$ MAX (Task$_i$)

Sketch 7.5 Execution time in single thread vs. multi-thread parallelism

Thread Synchronization

If multiple threads are using the same memory, there must be a synchronization system in place. Thread synchronization is hard because it involves locking of resources. If system is not implemented with high degree of thoughtful design then it can cause some intermittent problems that are why finding bugs and fixing thread synchronization related problems are very tough. There are many techniques used for thread synchronization; Critical section being the most important one if threads belong to the same process.

Thread synchronization in different processes are achieved using

- Event
- Mutex
- Semaphore

Cluster Computing

Cluster is a widely-used term meaning independent computers combined into a unified system through software and networking.

- Beowulf Clusters are scalable performance clusters based on commodity hardware, on a private system network, with open source software (Linux) infrastructure.
- MPI (Message Passing Interface) describes an API for allowing programs to communicate with their parallel components

Beowulf Cluster

Beowulf is a term associated with a cluster of computers interconnected with a network having following characteristics:

- Client nodes are set up in very dumb fashion
- Client nodes are commodity off the shelves (COTS) hardware
- Network is also COTS (network file system)
- Nodes run open source software
- User starts programs on master machine
- Scripts use rsh to invoke subprograms on worker nodes

Recipe to create a Beowulf cluster

- Buy a bunch of MCOTS (Mass Market Commodity-Off-The-Shelf) PC's for ``nodes". Details (graphics adapter or no, processor speed and family, amount of memory, UP or SMP, presence and size of disk) unimportant, as long as they ``work" in the configuration purchased
- Add a nice, cheap 100BT Network Interface Card (NIC) to each. Connect each NIC to nice, cheap 100BT switch to interconnect all nodes
- Add Linux and various Beowulf packages to support distributed parallel computing; PVM, MPI, MOSIX, maybe more
- Blow your code away by running it in parallel

Open Source Message Passing Interface (Open MPI)

The Open MPI project (http://www.open-mpi.org/) is an open source implementation of MPI library. Open MPI project consists of many sub-systems primarily:

- OMPI – Open MPI core library
- ORTE – Open run time environment
- OPAL – Open portable access layer

These three sub-systems have strict dependencies between them. OMPI depends on ORTE and ORTE depends on OPAL.

Open MPI Essentials

Communicator
- Processes are represented by a unique "rank" (integer) and ranks are numbered 0, 1, 2, ..., N-1. MPI_COMM_WORLD means "all the processes in the MPI application." It is called a communicator and it provides all information necessary to do message passing.

Enter & Exit
- MPI_Init(&argc, &argv);
- MPI_Finalize();

Process rank and size
- A process in a parallel application needs to know who it is (its rank) and how many other processes exist. A process finds out its own rank by calling MPI_Comm_rank():

- The total number of processes is returned by PI_Comm_size():

Sending Message
- A message is an array of elements of a given datatype. MPI supports all the basic datatypes and allows a more elaborate application to construct new datatypes at runtime. A message is sent to a specific process and is marked by a tag (integer value) specified by the user. Tags are used to distinguish between different message types a process might send/receive. In the sample code above, the tag is used to distinguish between work and termination messages.
- MPI_Send(buffer, count, datatype, destination, tag, MPI_COMM_WORLD);

Receiving Message
- A receiving process specifies the tag and the rank of the sending process. MPI_ANY_TAG and MPI_ANY_SOURCE may be used optionally to receive a message of any tag and from any sending process.
- MPI_Recv(buffer, maxcount, datatype, source, tag, MPI_COMM_WORLD, &status); Information about the received message is returned in a status variable. The received message tag is status.MPI_TAG and the rank of the sending process is status.MPI_SOURCE.

Process spawning

- User explicitly spawns child processes to do work
- MPI library aware of the number of available machines
- MPI system will spawn processes on different machines

Shared memory

- MPI programs define a "Window" of a certain size as a shared memory region
- Multiple processes attach to the window
- Get() and Put() primitives copy data into the shared memory asynchronously
- Fence() command blocks until all users of the window reach the fence, at which point their shared memories are consistent

- User is responsible for ensuring that stale data is not read from shared memory buffer

Synchronization

- Supports intuitive notion of "barriers" with Fence()
- Mutual exclusion locks also supported
- Library ensures that multiple machines cannot access the lock at the same time
- Ensuring that failed nodes cannot deadlock an entire distributed process will increase system complexity

Communication

- Basic communication unit in MPI is a message – a piece of data sent from one machine to another
- MPI provides message-sending and receiving functions that allow processes to exchange messages in a thread-safe fashion over the network
- Multi-Party Messages

Functional Programming Overview

Functional programming requires that functions are first-class, which means that they are treated like any other values and can be passed as arguments to other functions or be returned as a result of a function. Being first-class also means that it is possible to define and manipulate functions from within other functions. Special attention needs to be given to functions that reference local variables from their scope. If such a function escapes their block after being returned from it, the local variables must be retained in memory, as they might be needed later when the function is called.

Functional programs such as Scala are typically smaller (by a factor of two to ten). Since they are smaller, they tend to be less error-prone.

Features of Functional Programming

- Focus on "what" should be done, but not necessarily "how" For example, in SQL, we do not specify the order of JOINs, SELECTs, or WHEREs. The SQL engine in the RDBMS does all that for us.
- Higher Order Functions; A higher-order function is a function that takes other functions as arguments or returns a function as result. Map() and fold() are two good examples.
- Pure functions; Area = PI * (R**2)
- The order of function invocation does not matter.
- Functions can use lazy evaluation.
- Functions can be optimized.
- Refactoring and testing is easier.
- Immutable data; Immutable variables makes parallel execution easier. XSLT transformations are an example of a language with immutable variables. Spreadsheets are another example of functional programming with immutable variables.

Higher order Function

Map (map is the name of a higher-order function that applies a given function to a sequence of elements (such as a list) and returns a sequence of results.) Here's a quick example in Ruby of a higher order function, "select". It returns all items matching a logical expression that is passed into "select" as an argument.

numbers = [1,2,3,4,5,6,7];

evens = numbers.select{|x| x % 2 == 0}

puts evens #=> [2, 4, 6]

Lazy evaluation

Lazy evaluation in computer science refers to a technique in which only data that is needed at the execution time is read and produced. For example, the unix "grep" command will normally find all occurrences of a string. But if it knows the "head" program will only print the first three, "grep" can stop after the first three and not find the remaining strings.

grep database files.txt | head 3

Exercise

RMI exercise

Consider a distributed system architecture where a server provides a service for calculating square of a number. The interface description for the server is as below:

```
import java.rmi.*;

interface SquareOne extends Remote {
   long square(int i) throws RemoteException;
}
```

The server class implements this method; the main method starts the server

```
import java.rmi.*;
import java.rmi.server.*;
import java.rmi.registry.*;
import java.net.*;

public class Square extends UnicastRemoteObject implements
SquareOne {

   Square() throws RemoteException { }

   public long square(int x) throws RemoteException {
      return x*x;
   }

   public static void main(String[] args) {
      System.setSecurityManager(new RMISecurityManager());
      try {
         Square s = new Square();
         Naming.bind("//localhost:2013/Square", s);
         System.out.println("Computing squares");
      } catch(Exception e) {
         e.printStackTrace();
      }
   }
}
```

The client calculates the square of first ten numbers using the remote service:

```
import java.rmi.*;
import java.rmi.registry.*;

public class SquareClient {
```

```
   public static void main(String[] args) {
      System.setSecurityManager(new RMISecurityManager());
      try {
         SquareOne t = (SquareOne)Naming.lookup(
"//localhost:2013/Square");
         for(int i = 0; i < 10; i++)
            System.out.println("Square" +"("+i+") = " +
t.square(i));
      } catch(Exception e) {
         e.printStackTrace();
      }
   }
}
```

Instructions:

1. Compile both client and server code.
2. The server and client needs to communicate over network. In RMI, server and client do not communicate directly, they use skeleton and stub to communicate with each other. The Java RMI compiler rmic (http://docs.oracle.com/javase/1.4.2/docs/tooldocs/solaris/rmic.html) generates skeleton and stub for you.

   >>rmic Square

3. In a general RMI scenario, there will be lot of services provided by different objects. Each server should register itself at a registry and clients can do service lookup at the registry for the services they need. For this, the registry itself should be started. This is done by the command:

   >>rmiregistry

4. After starting the rmiregistry, the server code has to be called as a new process. To access the socket for connection, a policy file can be used to grant permissions.

   >>java -Djava.security.policy=Square.policy Square

5. Similarly, client has to be invoked as a new process:

   >>java -Djava.security.policy=Square.policy SquareClient

6. If you find that this results in an error, you should change the port number(//hostname:port/ClassName) in the above code, compile it, and start rmiregistry at the new port number.

For Eg: >>rmiregistry 5000

MPI Exercise

#include <stdio.h>

#include <mpi.h>

int

main(int argc, char *argv[])

{

int rank, size;

MPI_Init(&argc, &argv);

MPI_Comm_rank(MPI_COMM_WORLD, &rank);

MPI_Comm_size(MPI_COMM_WORLD, &size);

printf("Hello world! I am %d of %d\n", rank, size);

MPI_Finalize();

return 0;

}

Compile
mpicc -o hello_world hello_world.c

Run
linux:~> mpirun -np 4 hello_world
Hello world from process 1 of 4
Hello world from process 2 of 4
Hello world from process 3 of 4
Hello world from process 0 of 4

Cyber Security

Chapter Goal

After studying this chapter, you should be able to:

- Learn about the various information security threats to internetworked enterprise software application and their impact to the business
- Learn how to create secure enterprise information

Introduction to Cyber Security

Cyber security is the collection of technologies, standards, policies and management practices that are applied to information to keep it secure. Cyber security underpins the commercial viability and profitability of enterprises of all sizes and the effectiveness of public sector organizations. This chapter begins by explaining why information security and its management are important for any modern organization. The chapter continues by examining the value that can be placed on information as an organizational asset.

Information security protects information (and the facilities and systems that store, use and transmit it) from a wide range of threats, in order to preserve its value to an organization. This definition of information security is adapted from that of the American National Security Telecommunications and Information Systems Security Committee (NSTISSC). There are two important characteristics of information that determine its value to an organization:

- Scarcity of the information outside the organization;

- Shareability of the information within the organization, or some part of it.

Simplifying somewhat, these characteristics state that information is only valuable if it provides advantage or utility to those who have it, compared with those who don't. Thus the value of any piece of information relates to its levels of share ability and scarcity. The aim of information security is to preserve the value of information by ensuring that these levels are correctly identified and preserved. Threats to information influence the organization's ability to share it within, or to preserve its scarcity outside. And threats that are carried out can cost millions in compensation and reputation, and may even jeopardize an institution's ability to survive. Here are some examples in which the making available of information that should have been kept scarce or the restricting of information that should have been shareable has damaged an organization.

Why security is important?

In today's high technology environment, organizations are becoming more and more dependent on their information systems. The public is increasingly concerned about the proper use of information, particularly personal data. The threats to information systems from criminals and terrorists are increasing. Many organizations will identify information as an area of their operation that needs to be protected as part of their system of internal control.

Example 1: Softbank – theft of consumer data for extortion

Softbank of Japan offers broadband internet services across Japan through two subsidiaries – Yahoo! BB and Softbank BB. In February 2004, the bank announced that the security of 4.5 million customer records had been compromised: data from both subsidiaries had been illegally copied and disseminated. The leaked details included customer names, home phone numbers, addresses and email IDs, but did not include passwords, access logs or credit card details.

Softbank became aware of the problem only when they were approached by two groups of extortionists. The criminals produced apparently genuine customer data and threatened that all of the data would be posted to the internet if they were not paid a large sum of money.

Japanese police made three arrests but suspected that there may have been connections to organized crime and the political far-right. Amazingly, the police concluded that there had in fact been two simultaneous, yet independent, extortion attempts against Softbank, both of them masterminded by employees of the company. All of the people accused of extortion had been authorized to access the customer data; but it appeared that Softbank had inadequate procedures to protect against its unwarranted copying and dissemination.

The bank immediately announced a tightening of security, further restricting access to their systems and enforcing tighter security on all of their subsidiaries. Profuse apologies were offered to the affected customers and ¥4 billion (£20 million) were paid in compensation. Furthermore, Softbank BB's president, Masayoshi Son, announced that he and other senior executives would take a 50 per cent pay cut for the next six months.

In this example, the threat was to reduce the value of an organization by revealing information that should have been a well-kept secret – scarce-within as well as scarce-without. It cost the company £20 million in compensation and affected its reputation.

Example 2: UCSF Medical Center

In October 2002, the University of California, San Francisco (UCSF) Medical Center received an email message from someone who claimed to be a doctor working in Pakistan and who threatened to release patient records onto the internet unless money owing to her was paid. Several confidential medical transcripts were attached to the email.

UCSF staff was mystified; they had no dealings in Pakistan and certainly did not employ the person who sent the email. The Medical Center began an immediate investigation, concentrating on their transcription service, which had been outsourced to Transcription Stat, based in nearby Sausalito. It transpired that Transcription Stat farmed out work to some fifteen subcontractors scattered across America. One of these subcontractors was Florida-based Sonya Newburn, who in turn employed further subcontractors, including one Tom Spires of Texas. No one at Transcription Stat realized that Spires also employed his own subcontractors, including the sender of the email. The sender alleged that Spires owed her money, and had not paid her for some time.

Newburn eventually agreed to pay the $500 that the email sender claimed was owed to her. In return the sender informed UCSF that she had had no intention of publicizing personal information and had destroyed any records in her care. Of course, there is no way to prove that the records have actually been destroyed.

Naturally, you would not wish your own medical records to be publicized: they should be scarce. This threat cost the organization little in money terms, but how much in reputation? Just what is a reputation worth? Or, to put it another way, how much is it worth paying in information security to protect a reputation?

Example 3: Logic bombs

In May 2000, Timothy Lloyd was found guilty of causing between $10 million and $12 million worth of damage to Omega Engineering, an American company specializing in precision engineering for clients, including the US Navy and NASA. Lloyd had been employed with Omega for 11 years, rising to the post of system administrator, and was responsible not only for the day-to-day operation of the company's computers but also for their disaster-recovery process.

In 1996, Lloyd became aware that he was about to be sacked and wrote a logic bomb – a six-line destructive program –, which he installed, on Omega's servers. Ten days later, Lloyd was dismissed and his logic bomb exploded, destroying company contracts and proprietary software used by Omega's manufacturing tools. Although Omega had instituted a backup procedure, Lloyd's account privileges had allowed him to disable these recovery systems. The damage done by his logic bomb was permanent.

When the logic bomb 'exploded' it wiped out information that was needed for the company to operate. As a result of lost business, Omega was forced to lay off some 80 employees and found it rewriting the very software that had once given it a competitive edge over its rivals. In effect, what Lloyd managed to do, in the most decisive way possible, was to prevent vital information being shared.

Information Security- a holistic approach

Information can only be protected within an enterprise with a holistic approach. This includes designing all three kinds of security as given below.

- Physical Security
- Technological Security
  - Application Security
  - Operating System Security
  - Network Security
- Policies and Procedures

Physical Security

- Limit access to physical space to prevent asset theft and unauthorized entry
- Protecting against information leakage and document theft Ex: Dumpster Diving - gathering sensitive information by sifting through the company's garbage

Technological- Application Security

Securing application using firewall is a common and popular practice within enterprises. Firewall provides specialized, layered application threat protection for medium and large enterprises, application service providers, and SaaS providers. A web application firewall protects your web-based applications and internet-facing data from attack and data loss. Modern firewall appliances use advanced techniques to provide bidirectional protection against malicious sources, application layer DoS attacks and sophisticated threats like SQL injection and Cross-site scripting. The application security process may include:

- Identity verification process
- Server configuration
- Data Interpretation

A secure business application must be protected for different types of attacks at each tier.

A secure eBusiness application

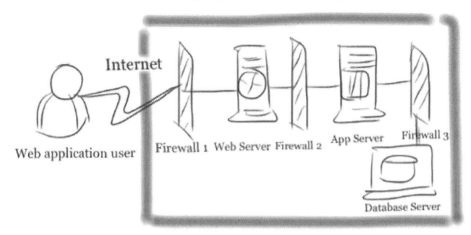

Sketch 8.1 A 3 tier eBusiness application secured with firewalls

Tips for securing web application

Use Application Firewall

Application firewall protects the web components from processing malicious data. The most common forms of malicious data are buffer overflows and cross-site scripting attacks (XSS links), either through script injection in valid pages or redirection to other Web sites. Once firewall is enabled, you can also track firewall activity by checking the log file, which generates rejection requests.

Configure Cryptography

Secure temporary files

Web application might use temporary files during its server activities. These files may not be encrypted and may expose sensitive data. Implement the following measures to secure temporary files:

- Restrict access to the temporary files directory.
- Grant read and writes permissions for the temp directory only to the web application account. Deny all other accounts any access.
- Enable encryption of temporary files. Because encrypted content is unintelligible, it is useless for potential attackers. Encrypting temporary files may affect performance.

Secure application data and content

- Secure the database and the database API using the mechanisms provided by the database, the network, and the operating system.
- Assign a limited number of users to maintain the database.
- Use your database native security to grant only minimum permissions to the user accounts that access the database
- Limit the number of users who have read or write access for the Content

Technological - OS Security

The operating system is the physical environment where your application runs. Any vulnerability in the operating system could compromise the security of the application. By securing the operating system, you make the environment stable, control access to resources, and control external access to the environment.

The physical security of the system is essential. Threats can come through the Web, but they can also come from a physical terminal. Even if the Web access is very secure, if an attacker obtains physical access to a server, breaking into a system is much easier. Here are some tips for securing operating system in each category:

User Accounts

- Limit the number of user accounts on the server computers.
- Unnecessary and legacy user accounts increase system complexity and may present system vulnerabilities, review and eliminate them.
- Ensure that only a few trusted users have administrative access to the server computers. Fewer administrators make it easier to maintain accountability. The administrators must be competent.
- Assign the minimum required access permissions for the account that runs the application. If attackers obtain access to the application, they have the permissions of the user who runs the application.

Account Policies

- Develop and administer password policies that promote operating system security. Examples of such policies are the strong password rule and the password change schedule.

- Test the strength of users' passwords by breaking the passwords. The users who do not comply with the strong password rule receive a notification to update their passwords according to the organization password policy.

- On a UNIX operating system, activate the shadow password file. On UNIX, passwords are stored in the /etc/passwd file. This file is open to everyone, which presents a security risk. To enhance password security, activate the shadow password file named /etc/shadow. If this file is available, passwords are stored in it instead of the passwd file. Because permissions for the /etc/shadow file are more restrictive, the security risk is lower.

File System

- Grant the users read-only permissions for required directories. If attackers obtain access to an application, they have the user permissions.

- Deny access by default. Access to resources is denied for everyone except for the users to whom access is granted explicitly. You can deny read and write permissions for all directory structures for all users. Only users to whom these permissions are granted explicitly have access to the directories and files. This policy also protects any resources that were overlooked by an administrator.

Network Services

- Provide the minimum number of required services on the server computer. Use only the services that you need to run the application. Each service is a potential entry point for a malicious attack. Reducing the number of running services also makes your system more manageable. For example, you may not need the ftp, rlogin, or ssh services.

- Reduce the level of access permissions for the network services users. Network services are exposed to the public.

- Ensure that the user accounts that have access to the Web server do not have access to the shell functions.

- Ensure that unused services do not exist in the rc files, rc0 through to rc6, in the /etc directory on UNIX and Linux operating systems.
- Ensure that unused services are not running, and that they do not start automatically on Microsoft Windows operating systems.
- Ensure that required services are running on UNIX. You can use the ps and netstat utilities to see the running services. The ps utility gives a list of processes currently running on the computer. The netstat utility provides a list of ports that are currently in use.
- Reduce the number of trusted ports specified in the /etc/services file. Delete or comment out the ports that you do not plan to use to eliminate possible entry points to the system.
- Protect your system against NetBIOS threats associated with ports 137, 138, and 139. These ports are listed in the /etc/services file.
- Use wrapper services, such as iptables.
- Ensure that the services are current by checking often for security updates.
- Avoid using services that have a graphical user interface (GUI), if possible. Such services introduce many known security vulnerabilities.

System Patches

- Run the latest, vendor-recommended patches for the operating system. The patches may be core OS patches, or patches required by additional applications.
- Schedule regular maintenance of security patches.

Operating System Minimization

- Remove nonessential applications to reduce possible system vulnerabilities.
- Restrict local services to the services required for operation.
- Implement protection for buffer overflow. You may need third-party software to do this.

Logging and Monitoring

- Log security-related events, including successful and failed logons, logoffs, and changes to user permissions.

- Monitor system log files.
- Use a time server to correlate time for forensics.
- Secure the system log files by restricting access permissions to them. Logs are important for daily maintenance and as a disaster recovery tool. Therefore, they must be protected from system failures and user tampering.
- Secure the logging configuration file. The configuration file contains settings that, if changed, can compromise the reliability of the log system. For example, setting the log level incorrectly may cause some failures not to be logged.
- Enable logging of access requests on the Web server. This can be useful in identifying malicious activity.

System Integrity

- Build production systems from a known and repeatable process to ensure the system integrity.
- Check systems periodically against snapshots of the original system.
- Use available third-party auditing software to check the system integrity.
- Back up the system resources on a regular basis.

Technological – Network Security

The network is the entry point to an application. Therefore, the network security mechanisms are the first line of defense against potential threats from the outside. Network security involves protecting the protocols and the communication channels, as well as devices, such as the router, the firewall, and the switch.

Tips for securing your network

- Use a firewall. This will allow only legitimate access to the network.
- Ensure that the firewall provides packet forwarding and filtering. These firewall features introduce an additional layer of protection. Forwarding packets prevents the outside world from direct contact with the computers inside the protected network. Filtering can block some types of requests, or requests that come from some domains or IP addresses.

These techniques help to reduce the number of illegitimate requests that can be passed to the internal network.

- Limit the number of accessible ports.
- Limit the traffic direction on some ports.
- Limit some network protocols, such as ping.

Web Servers

- Remove any unused virtual directories.
- Remove or disable example default cgi-bin or ASP scripts provided with your web server application. For example: Apache: cgi-bin/printenv.pl.
- Grant read, write, and execute permissions explicitly for each Web site and virtual directory.
- Create a root directory for the Web server.
- Ensure that access permissions for the physical files are set up properly. Only some users require read and write permissions for these files.
- Remove unwanted default mappings, such as for applications with the .htr, .idc, .stm, .printer, and .htw file extensions.
- Enable secure sockets layer (SSL) on the Web server. SSL is used to encrypt a user's communication with the Web server. For more information, see the section about configuring the Web server in the IBM Cognos Business Intelligence Installation and Configuration Guide.

Passive attacks

A **passive attack** is characterized by the interception of messages without modification. There is no change to the network data or systems. The message itself may be read or its occurrence may simply be logged. Identifying the communicating parties and noting the duration and frequency of messages can be of significant value in itself. From this knowledge certain deductions or inferences may be drawn regarding the likely subject matter, the urgency or the implications of messages being sent. This type of activity is termed **traffic analysis**. Because there may be no evidence that an attack has taken place, prevention is a priority. Traffic analysis, however, may be a legitimate management activity because of the need to collect data showing usage of services, for instance. Some interception of traffic may also be considered necessary by governments and law enforcement agencies interested in the surveillance of criminal, terrorist and other activities. These agencies may have privileged physical access to sites and computer systems.

Active attacks

An **active attack** is one in which an unauthorized change of the system is attempted. This could include, for example, the modification of transmitted or stored data, or the creation of new data streams. Figure 2 (see Section 3.2) shows four sub-categories here: masquerade or fabrication, message replay, message modification and denial of service or interruption of availability.

Masquerade attacks, as the name suggests, relate to an entity (usually a computer or a person) taking on a false identity in order to acquire or modify information, and in effect achieve an unwarranted privilege status. Masquerade attacks can also incorporate other categories.

Message replay involves the re-use of captured data at a later time than originally intended in order to repeat some action of benefit to the attacker: for example, the capture and replay of an instruction to transfer funds from a bank account into one under the control of an attacker. This could be foiled by confirmation of the freshness of a message.

Message modification could involve modifying a packet header address for the purpose of directing it to an unintended destination or modifying the user data.

Denial-of-service attacks prevent the normal use or management of communication services, and may take the form of either a targeted attack on a particular service or a broad, incapacitating attack. For example, a network may be flooded with messages that cause a degradation of service or possibly a complete collapse if a server shuts down under abnormal loading. Another example is rapid and repeated requests to a web server, which bar legitimate access to others. Denial-of-service attacks are frequently reported for internet-connected services.

Because complete prevention of active attacks is unrealistic, a strategy of detection followed by recovery is more appropriate.

Threat of Virus

The word 'virus' is used collectively to refer to Trojans and worms, as well as more specifically to mean a particular type of worm. A **Trojan** is a program that has hidden instructions enabling it to carry out a malicious act such as the capture of passwords. These could then be used in other forms of attack. A **worm** is a program that can replicate itself and create a level of demand for services that cannot be satisfied. The term **virus** is also used for a worm that replicates by attaching itself to other programs.

Tapping into transmission media

Satellite, microwave and wireless transmissions can provide opportunities for passive attack, without much danger of an intruder being detected, because the environment at the point of intrusion is virtually unaffected by the eavesdropping activity. Satellite transmissions to earth generally have a wide geographic spread with considerable over-spill of the intended reception area. Although microwave links use a fairly focused beam of radiated energy, with appropriate technical know-how and some specialist equipment it is relatively straightforward physically to access the radiated signals.

Wireless LANs is another technology that creates vulnerabilities. . In general, detecting and monitoring unencrypted wireless transmissions is easy. You may have noticed that when you switch a mobile telephone handset on, an initialization process starts, during which your handset is authenticated and your location registered. The initial sequence of messages may be picked up by other circuits such as a nearby fixed telephone handset or a public address system, and is often heard as an audible signal. This indicates how easy it is to couple a wireless signal into another circuit. Sensing a communication signal may be relatively straightforward, but separating out a particular message exchange from a multiplex of many signals will be more difficult, especially when, as in mobile technology, frequency hopping techniques are employed to spread the spectrum of messages and so avoid some common transmission problems. However, to a determined attacker with the requisite knowledge, access to equipment and software tools, this is all possible.

Security Concepts

- Authentication

- Authorization
- Confidentiality
- Data / Message Integrity
- Accountability
- Availability

What is Authentication?

Authentication is needed to provide some assurance about the source of a message: did it originate from the location it appears to have originated from? One of the simplest authentication methods is the use of a shared secret such as a password. Assume that Alice and Bob share a password. Alice may challenge Bob to provide the shared password and if he does so correctly and Alice is confident that the password has not been compromised in any way, then she may be reassured that she is indeed communicating with Bob. Using the following steps, public key encryption can be used to provide an alternative challenge–response protocol between communicating entities that do not share a secret key:

- Alice challenges Bob by sending him some random number.
- Bob encrypts the random number using his own private key and sends the result to Alice.
- Alice decrypts the message using Bob's public key. If the result matches her original random value and if she has confidence that the public key does indeed belong to Bob, then she may be assured that it is Bob who has sent the message to her.

What is a digital signature?

In effect, when a message is encrypted with a private key, the key acts like the signature of the owner. As long as the key has not been compromised in any way it will act as an assurance of the authenticity of the message. However, Bob would be ill-advised to sign a document unless he was very sure about its contents. What if the value sent by Alice was not, after all, some random number but instead was an encrypted message giving instructions to Bob's bank to transfer funds into Alice's account? A better way for Bob to provide authentication when sending messages to Alice would be for him to create a digest of his message encrypted with his private key and to append this to the message he sends to Alice. On receipt Alice could create a new digest using an identical algorithm and compare this with the decrypted digest sent by Bob. If the two match and she is confident that Bob's private key has not been compromised in any way she may feel reasonably confident that the message did originate with Bob. Such an encrypted message digest is known as a **digital signature**.

What are the authentication methods available?

- Something you know (i.e., Passwords)
- Something you have (i.e., Tokens)
- Something you are (i.e., Biometrics)

Something you know

Example: Passwords
- Simple to implement
- Simple for users to understand
- Easy to crack (unless users choose strong ones)
- Passwords are reused many times
- One-time Passwords (OTP): different password used each time, but it is difficult for user to remember all of them

Something you have

- OTP Cards (e.g. SecurID): generates new password each time user logs in
- Smart Card: tamper-resistant, stores secret information, entered into a card-reader
- Token / Key (i.e., iButton)
- ATM Card
- Strength of authentication depends on difficulty of forging

Something you are - Biometrics

- Pros: "raises the bar"
- Cons: false negatives/positives, social acceptance, key management
- false positive: authentic user rejected

- false negative: impostor accepted

Technique	Effectiveness	Acceptance
Palm Scan	1	6
Iris Scan	2	1
Retinal Scan	3	7
Fingerprint	4	5
Voice Id	5	3
Facial Recognition	6	4
Signature Dynamics	7	2

What is Authorization?

- Checking whether a user has permission to conduct some action; Is a "subject" (Alice) allowed to access an "object" (open a file)?
- *Access Control List*: mechanism used by many operating systems to determine whether users are authorized to conduct different actions

What is an Access Control Lists (ACLs)?

- Set of three-tuples <User, Resource, Privilege>
- Specifies which users are allowed to access which resources with which privileges
- Privileges can be assigned based on roles (e.g. admin)

User	Resource	Privilege
Alice	/home/Alice /*	Read, write, execute
Bob	/home/Bob /*	Read, write, execute

What are Access Control Models?

- ACLs used to implement these models

- Mandatory: computer system decides exactly who has access to which resources
- Discretionary (e.g. UNIX): users are authorized to determine which other users can access files or other resources that they create, use, or own
- Role-Based (Non-Discretionary): user's access & privileges determined by role

Bell-LaPadula Model

Classifications:

- Top Secret
- Secret
- Confidential
- Unclassified

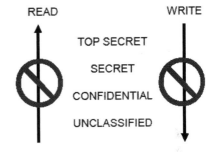

What is Confidentiality?

Confidentiality is about selecting who or what is allowed access to data and systems. This is achieved through encryption and access control systems. The goal is to keep the contents of communication or data on storage secret.

Example: Alice and Bob want their communications to be secret from eve droppers.

- Keep knowledge of the existence of data secure, this may be of significant value to an eavesdropper.
- Use keys – a secret shared between Alice & Bob Sometimes accomplished with Cryptography, Steganography, Access Controls, Database Views

Message/ Data Integrity

The integrity of data is maintained when modification is allowed only by authorized persons or organizations. The modifications could include any changes such as adding to, selectively deleting from, or even changing the status of a set of data.

Data Integrity means no corruption of data. It is also called "Man in the middle attack".

Example: Has Molly tampered with the message that Alice sends to Bob?

How do you maintain Message/Data Integrity?

Using Hash functions

A hash function is any well-defined procedure or mathematical function, which converts a large, possibly variable-sized amount of data into a small datum. The values returned by a hash function are called hash values, hash codes, hash sums, or simply hashes.

A cryptographic hash function is a deterministic procedure that takes an arbitrary block of data and returns a fixed-size bit string, the (cryptographic) hash value, such that an accidental or intentional change to the data will change the hash value. The data to be encoded is often called the "message", and the hash value is sometimes called the message digest. MD5 and SHA-1 are the most commonly used cryptographic hash functions in the field of Computer security.

MD5 (Message-Digest algorithm 5) is a widely used cryptographic hash function with a 128-bit hash value. The 128-bit MD5 hashes (also termed message digests) are represented as a sequence of 16 hexadecimal bytes. The following demonstrates a 40-byte ASCII input and the corresponding MD5 hash:

MD5 of "This is an example of an MD5 Hash Value." =
3413EE4F01F2A0AA17664088E79CF5C2

Even a small change in the message will result in a completely different hash. For example, changing the period at the end of the sentence to an exclamation mark:

MD5 of "This is an example of an MD5 Hash Value!" =
B872D23A7D14B6EE3B390A58C17F21A8

SHA stands for Secure Hash Algorithm. SHA-1 produces a 160-bit digest from a message and is represented as a sequence of 20 hexadecimal bytes. The following is an example of SHA-1 digests:

Just like MD5, even a small change in a message will result in a completely different hash. For example:

SHA1 of "This is a test." = AFA6C8B3A2FAE95785DC7D9685A57835D703AC88

SHA1 of "This is a pest." = FE43FFB3C844CC93093922D1AAC44A39298CAE11

Hash functions are used by Computer Forensic experts to:

- Authentication of data; proving that two things are same.
- Reduction of data; to exclude many known files from hundreds of thousands of files you have to look at
- Identification of data; to find needle in haystack

Summary of Hash functions

MD5

- output 128 bits
- collision resistance completely broken by researchers in China in 2004

SHA1

- output 160 bits
- no collision found yet, but method exist to find collisions in less than 2^{80}
- considered insecure for collision resistance

SHA2 (SHA-224, SHA-256, SHA-384, SHA-512)

- outputs 224, 256, 384, and 512 bits, respectively
- No real security concerns yet

Checksums and Cyclic Redundancy Code (CRC) for Data Integrity

Checksums or CRC are computation of check sequence when data is transmitted or received. Data is appended with check sequences and combined as code word before transmission. There are various types of checksums used such as:

- Integer addition "checksum"

- One's complement "checksum"
- Fletcher Checksum
- Adler Checksum
- ATN Checksum (AN/466)

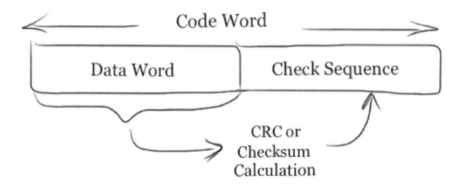

Sketch 8.2 Checksum for message/data integrity

To check data integrity:

- Code word is received or retrieved
- Compute CRC or checksum on the received data
- If computed value equals check sequence then no data corruption found (at least not detected)

CRC and checksums are used in:

- Network packet integrity check
- Image integrity check for software update
- Boot-up integrity check for program image(corrupted boot record)
- RAM value integrity check

What is data corruption?

Data corruption happens when a bit is flipped. Bit flip is also known as bisymmetric inversions. Each bit has some probability of being inverted. The number of bits flipped in an error word is known as "Weight" of error word (number of "1" bits in error).

Message Authentication Codes (MACs) Different From Confidentiality

MAC is a function of the message and a secret key that produces a fixed-length value that serves as the authenticator. This technique assumes that two communicating parties, say A and B, share a common secret key K. When A has a message to send to B, it calculates the MAC as a function of the message and the key:

MAC = C(K, M), where

M = input message

C = MAC function

K = shared secret key

MAC = message authentication code

The receiver is assured that the message has not been altered. If an attacker alters the message but does not alter the MAC, then the receiver's calculation of the MAC will differ from the received MAC. Because the attacker is assumed not to know the secret key, the attacker cannot alter the MAC to correspond to the alterations in the message.

The receiver is assured that the message is from the alleged sender. Because no one else knows the secret key, no one else could prepare a message with a proper MAC.

Accountability

Accountability in IT security context refers to be able to log the activities and keep the audit trails. By having accountability methods in place, an attacker cannot cover his tracks.

- Logging & Audit Trails
- Secure Time stamping (OS vs. Network)
- Data integrity in logs & audit trails, must not be able to change trails, or be able to detect changes to logs

Availability

It is about uptime, Free Storage of resources such as web servers. Examples; dial tone availability, system downtime limit, web server response time

Solutions

- Add redundancy (replication) to remove single point of failure
- Impose "limits" that legitimate users can use. Goal of DoS (Denial of Service) attacks are to reduce availability. Malware used to send excessive traffic to victim site. Overwhelmed servers can't process legitimate traffic

Introduction to Firewalls

Firewalls play an important role in restricting and controlling access to networks. A firewall is normally implemented within a router or gateway, and will monitor incoming and outgoing traffic at the boundary of the protected zone. It is a device that denies external hosts access to selected insecure services within the protected zone (e.g. denial of dial-in services), while also denying internal hosts access to insecure services outside the protected zone. There may be further control within the protected zone, for example to limit access from one internal LAN segment to another.

A firewall provides the means to implement some of an organization's network security policies and may be transparent to users of the network in terms of its presence and the level of inconvenience caused. This depends on the type of firewall and the policies that are implemented.

Types of firewalls

- Packet-filtering routers
- Firewall gateways (Application level gateways)
- Circuit-level gateways
- Combination of all 3 above is called dynamic packet filter

Packet filtering routers

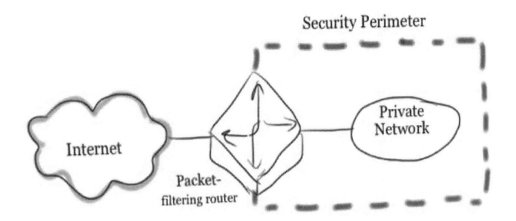

Sketch 8.3   Firewall – Packet filtering

How to configure a packet filtering router?

1. Start with a security policy
2. Specify allowable packets in terms of logical expressions on packet fields
3. Rewrite expressions in syntax supported by your vendor
4. General rules – start with least privilege. All that is not expressly permitted is prohibited. If you do not need it, eliminate it

Firewall - Stateful Packet Filtering

A traditional packet filter makes filtering decisions on an individual packet basis and does not take into consideration any higher layer context. A stateful inspection packet filter tightens up the rules for TCP traffic by creating a directory of outbound TCP connections, and will allow incoming traffic to high-numbered ports only for those packets that fit the profile of one of the entries in this directory. Hence they are better able to detect bogus packets sent out of context.

Firewall Gateways

Firewall gateways are Network Address Translation (NAT) box like a home router.

Firewall runs set of proxy programs. These proxies filter incoming, outgoing packets. The filtering policy is embedded in the proxy code. There are two kinds of proxies:

- Application-level gateways/proxies which is tailored to http, ftp, smtp, etc.
- Circuit-level gateways/proxies which is TCP level

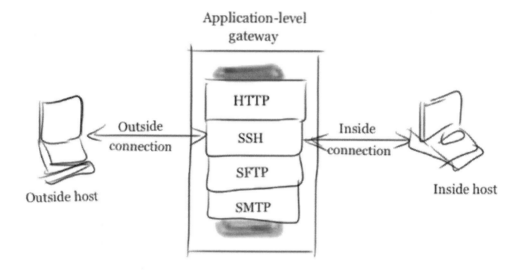

Sketch 8.4 Application level gateway

Circuit level gateway

Circuit level gateways are specialized function performed by an Application-level Gateway. The gateway typically relays TCP segments from one connection to the other without examining the contents. The security function consists of determining which connections will be allowed.

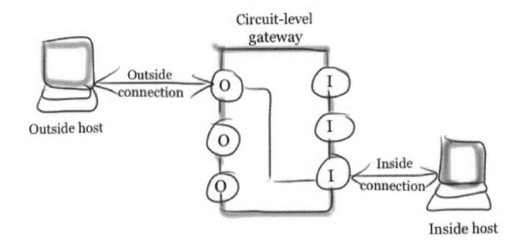

Sketch 8.5   Circuit level gateway

Introduction to Encryption and Cryptography

Encryption is a process that transforms information (the **plaintext**) into a seemingly unintelligible form (the **ciphertext**) using a mathematical algorithm and some secret information (the encryption **key**). The process of **decryption** undoes this transformation using a mathematical algorithm, in conjunction with some secret value (the decryption key) that reverses the effects of the encryption algorithm. An encryption algorithm and all its possible keys, plaintexts and ciphertexts are known as a **cryptosystem** or cryptographic system.

Cryptography is the general name given to the art and science of keeping messages secret. It is not the purpose here to examine in detail any of the mathematical algorithms that are used in the cryptographic process, but instead to provide a general overview of the process and its uses.

Modern encryption systems use mathematical algorithms that are well known and have been exposed to public testing, relying for security on the keys used. For example, a well-known and very simple algorithm is the **Caesar cipher**, which encrypts each letter of the alphabet by shifting it forward three places. Thus A becomes D, B becomes E, C becomes F and so on. A cipher that uses an alphabetic shift for any number of places is also commonly referred to as a Caesar cipher, although this isn't strictly correct since the Caesar cipher is technically one in which each character is replaced by one three places to the right. This could be described mathematically as $p + 3 = c$, where p is the plaintext and c the ciphertext. For a more general equation you could write $p + x = c$ where x could take any integer value up to 25. Selecting different values for x would obviously produce different values for c, although the basic algorithm of a forward shift is unchanged. Thus, in this example the value x is the key. (The Caesar cipher is of course too simple to be used for practical security systems.)

There are two main requirements for cryptography:

1. It should be computationally infeasible to derive the plaintext from the ciphertext without knowledge of the decryption key.
2. It should be computationally infeasible to derive the ciphertext from the plaintext without knowledge of the encryption key.

Both these conditions should be satisfied even when the encryption and decryption algorithms themselves are known.

Modern encryption systems are derived from one of two basic systems: symmetric key (sometimes called shared key) systems, and asymmetric key (often called public key) systems.

What is a symmetric key (Shared Key) system?

We can think of **symmetric key systems** as sharing a single secret key between the two communicating entities. This key is used for both encryption and decryption. (In practice, the encryption and decryption keys are often different but it is relatively straightforward to calculate one key from the other.) It is common to refer to these two entities as Alice and Bob because this simplifies the descriptions of the transactions, but you should be aware that these entities are just as likely to be software applications or hardware devices as individuals.

Symmetric key systems rely on using some secure method whereby Alice and Bob can first agree on a secret key that is known only to them. When Alice wants to send a private message to some other entity, says Charlie, another secret key must first be shared. If Bob then wishes to communicate privately with Charlie himself, he and Charlie require a separate secret key to share. Figure 5 is a graphical representation of the keys Alice, Bob and Charlie would each need if they were to send private messages to each other. As you can see from this, for a group of three separate entities to send each other private messages, three separate shared keys are required.

Components of Symmetric key system

A **block cipher** operates on groups of bits – typically groups of 64. If the final block of the plaintext message is shorter than 64 bits, it is padded with some regular pattern of 1s and 0s to make a complete block. Block ciphers encrypt each block independently, so the plaintext does not have to be processed in a sequential manner. This means that as well as allowing parallel processing for faster throughput, a block cipher also enables specific portions of the message (e.g. specific records in a database) to be extracted and manipulated. A block of plaintext will always encrypt to the same block of ciphertext provided that the same algorithm and key are used.

A **stream cipher** generally operates on one bit of plaintext at a time, although some stream ciphers operate on bytes. A component called a keystream generator generates a sequence of bits, usually known as a **keystream**. In the simplest form of stream cipher, a modulo-2 adder (exclusive-OR or XOR gate) combines each bit in the plaintext with each bit in the keystream to produce the ciphertext. At the receiving end, another modulo-2 adder combines the ciphertext with the keystream to recover the plaintext. This is illustrated in Figure 6. The encryption of a unit of plain text is dependent on its position in the data stream, so identical units of plaintext will not always encrypt to identical units of ciphertext when using the same algorithm and key.

A selection of some symmetric key systems used in popular software products is given in Table 2.

Table 2: Examples of commercial symmetric key systems

Algorithm	Description
DES (Data Encryption Standard)	A block cipher with a 56-bit key. Adopted in 1977 by the US National Security Agency (NSA) as the US Federal standard, it has been one of the most widely used encryption algorithms but, as computers have become more powerful, it is now considered to have become too weak.
Triple-DES (or 3DES)	A variant of DES developed to increase its security. It

Algorithm	Description
	has several forms; each operates on a block three times using the DES algorithm, thus effectively increasing the key length. Some variants can use three different keys, the same key three times, or use an encryption–decryption–encryption mode.
IDEA(International Data Encryption Algorithm)	A block cipher with a 128-bit key published in 1990. It encrypts data faster than DES and is considered to be a more secure algorithm.
Blowfish	A compact and simple block cipher with a variable-length key of up to 448 bits.
RC2 (Rivest cipher no. 2)	A block cipher with a variable-length key of up to 2048 bits. The details of the algorithm used have not been officially published.
RC4 (Rivest cipher no. 4)	A stream cipher with a variable-length key of up to 2048 bits.

Often the key length for RC2 and RC4 is limited to 40 bits because of the US export approval process. A shorter key reduces the strength of an encryption algorithm.

What is Asymmetric key (Public key) system?

Asymmetric or **public key systems** are based on encryption techniques whereby data that has been encrypted by one key can be decrypted by a different, seemingly unrelated key. One of the keys is known as the **public key** and the other is known as the **private key**. The keys are, in fact, related to each other mathematically but this relationship is complex, so that it is computationally infeasible to calculate one key from the other. Thus, anyone possessing only the public key is unable to derive the private key. They are able to encrypt messages that can be decrypted with the private key, but are unable to decrypt any messages already encrypted with the public key.

Each communicating entity will have its own key pair; the private key will be kept secret but the public key will be made freely available. For example, Bob, the owner of a key pair, could send a copy of his public key to everyone he knows, he could enter it into a public database, or he could respond to individual requests from entities wishing to communicate by sending his public key to them. But he would keep his private key secret. For Alice to send a private message to Bob, she first encrypts it using Bob's easily accessible public key. On receipt, Bob decrypts the ciphertext with his secret private key and recovers the original message. No one other than Bob can decrypt the ciphertext because only Bob has the private key and it is computationally infeasible to derive the private key from the public key. Thus, the message can be sent secretly from Alice to Bob without the need for the prior exchange of a secret key.

Using asymmetric key systems with n communicating entities, the number of key pairs required is n. Compare this with the number of shared keys required for symmetric key systems where the number of keys is related to the square of the number of communicating entities. Asymmetric key systems are therefore more scalable.

Public key algorithms can allow either the public key or the private key to be used for encryption with the remaining key used for decryption. This allows these particular public key algorithms to be used for authentication, as you will see later.

Public key algorithms place higher demands on processing resources than symmetric key algorithms and so tend to be slower. Public key encryption is therefore often used just to exchange a temporary key for a symmetric encryption algorithm. As with symmetric key systems, there are many public key algorithms available for use, although most of them are block ciphers. Two used in popular commercial software products are listed in Table 3.

Table 3: Examples of commercial asymmetric key systems

Algorithm	Description
RSA (named after its creators–Rivest, Shamir and Adleman)	A block cipher first published in 1978 and used for both encryption and authentication. Its security is based on the problem of factoring large integers, so any advances in the mathematical methods of achieving this will affect the algorithm's vulnerability.
DSS (Digital Signature Standard[1])	Developed by the US National Security Agency (NSA). Can be used only for digital signatures and not for encryption or key distribution.

Security Concepts in action

Case Study

- John works as Assistant manager at Retail store GoodBuy
- He logs on to B2B website for a TV manufacturer Vizio to order some TV sets which is going fast in his store.

Security

- John logs on to their https website

Availability

- Vizio ensures its web site is running 24-7

Authentication:

- John authenticates himself to the Vizio website

Confidentiality:

- John's browser and Vizio web server set up an encrypted connection (lock on bottom left of browser)

Authorization:

- Vizio web site consults database to check if John is authorized to order TVs on behalf of GoodBuy

Message / Data Integrity:

- Checksums are sent as part of each TCP/IP packets exchanged (+ SSL uses MACs)

Accountability:

- Vizio logs that John placed an order for Vizio LED 46" TV

Understanding Thefts

- Defacement
- Infiltration
- Phishing

- Pharming
- Insider Threats
- Click Fraud
- Denial of Service
- Data Theft/Loss

Defacement

Defacement is online Vandalism in which attackers get control of the web server and replace legitimate web pages with illegitimate ones.

Defacement attacks change the content or visual appearance of random websites; while the attackers are not doing this to make a direct profit, such attacks can damage the reputation of the organizations targeted, or cause financial losses. This type of attack is usually targeted towards political web sites. Defacement attack when happen to large high-profile companies, attackers not only sell the confidential data but also the tips on how to infect these company's web servers. In the past, cyber criminals were also able to start DoS attack after defacement.

What method do defacers use to exploit?

The defacers aren't selective in their targets; in most cases they just use scanners (automated tools) to find vulnerable servers, and automatically exploit them. The exploit automatically uploads a backdoor to the compromised server which will provide, for example, shell access to the compromised server.

Attackers also use "Google Dorks" to identify vulnerable servers. A "Google Dork" is a specially crafted search query which can be used, for example, to return results detailing all websites running a specific version of a specific application.

They use backdoor software to escalate privileges also known as "auto-rooters" or by extracting passwords from configuration files located on the compromised server. These so-called "auto- rooters" are simply shell scripts which will download an exploit pack containing precompiled exploits ready to be executed. The shell script will then analyze the machine in order to know which exploits to run, and run them. If the exploit successfully escalates privileges, another backdoor or rootkit will then be installed.

What are the solutions to defacement attacks?

In defacement attacks, attacker not only exploits technical vulnerabilities, but also exploits ignorance of system administrators. Most people who work with webservers today do not understand these various kinds of threats and how to keep the system up-to-date with security patches. Here are some tips to avoid and fight with defacement attacks:

- Keep your webservers up-to-date with OS/security patches.
- Do not assume that Linux/Unix operating system is safer than windows. You must go through the server hardening process to keep it secure
- Proper web server configuration is needed. In research and analysis, "File include" type vulnerabilities have been found to be the root cause. Attackers are able to insert any arbitrary file to initiate attack.

Infiltration

- Unauthorized parties gain access to resources of computer system (e.g. CPUs, disk, network bandwidth)
- Could gain read/write access to back-end DB
- Ensure that attacker's writes can be detected
- Different goals for different organizations
- Political site only needs integrity of data
- Financial site needs integrity & confidentiality

Phishing

Phishing is a type of deception designed to steal your valuable personal data, such as credit card numbers, passwords, account data, or other information. Con artists might send millions of fraudulent e-mail messages that appear to come from Web sites you trust, like your bank or credit card company, and request that you provide personal information. The term Phishing was coined from **Phreaking** (making phone calls for free back in 1970s.) and **Fishing** (using bait to lure the target).

- Attacker sets up spoofed site that looks real
- Lures users to enter login credentials and stores them

- Usually sent through an e-mail with link to spoofed site asking users to "verify" their account info
- The links might be disguised through the click texts
- Wary users can see actual URL if they hover over link

Here are some of the phrases to look for if you think email message is a phishing scam:

- "Verify your account." Businesses should not ask you to send passwords, login names, Social Security numbers, or other personal information through e-mail. If you receive an e-mail from anyone asking you to update your credit card information, do not respond: this is a phishing scam.
- "If you don't respond within 48 hours, your account will be closed." These messages convey a sense of urgency so that you'll respond immediately without thinking.

Phishers use a myriad of techniques to make their links and emails appear real. They are:

Misspelled ULRs

Misspelled URLs are probably the most popular form of deception because people tend to read the link so quickly that they barely notice that the URL is spelled incorrectly.

For example, the URL "www.microsoft.com" could appear instead as:

www.micosoft.com   www.mircosoft.com   www.verify-microsoft.com

Spoofing

One method of spoofing links used web addresses containing the @ symbol, which were used to include a username and password in a web URL. For example, the link http://www.google.com@members.tripod.com/ might deceive a casual observer into believing that the link will open a page on www.google.com, whereas the link actually directs the browser to a page on members.tripod.com, using a username of www.google.com; were there no such user, the page would open normally. (Wikipedia)

JavaScript

JavaScript, a web-based programming language is often used with legitimate webpages to do many different things; however, JavaScript can also be used to place a picture of the legitimate entity's URL over the address bar, or to close the original address bar and open a new one containing the legitimate URL.

Cross Site Scripting

In a cross site scripting "phish" an attacker uses a bank or service's own scripts against the victim. These types of attacks are particularly problematic, because they direct the user to sign in at their bank or service's own web page, where everything from the web address to the security certificates appears correct. In reality, the link to the website is crafted to carry out the attack, although it is very difficult to spot without specialist knowledge.

International Domain Names

Because many people are not as familiar with international web addresses, phishers can use this technique quite effectively. The fraudulent links might appear to be legitimate, but your browser might allow visually identical web addresses to lead to different, possibly malicious, websites

Pharming

There are two main ways through which "Pharmers" can execute their plan.

The first is through email viruses. A suspicious, but otherwise innocent email can contain an image that when viewed in your email program actually downloads a virus to your computer. The virus re-writes what is called a "host" file that normally converts the standard URL (www.ebay.com) into the numbers a computer understands (124.232.123.2). A computer with a compromised host file will go to the wrong website even if a user types in the correct URL.

The most malicious threat is **DNS "poisoning"** which can cause a large group of users to be herded to bogus sites. DNS; the domain name system translates web and e-mail addresses into numerical strings, acting as a sort of telephone directory for the internet. If a DNS directory is "poisoned" -- altered to contain false information regarding which web address is associated with what numeric string, users can be silently shuttled to a bogus website even if they type in the correct URL. (wired.com)

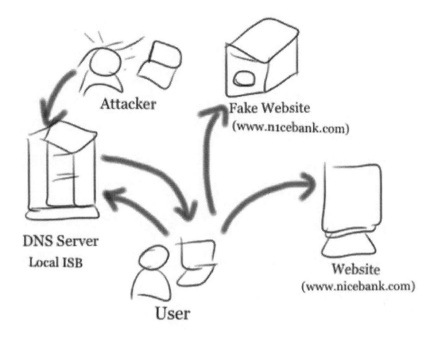

Sketch 8.6 DNS cache poisoning attack

How to prevent pharming?

In order to remove pharming as a threat, servers would have to add another layer of authentication. They would need to prove to you that they are who they say they are and establish a trusted link between you and them. That would require the site to obtain a certificate from a certificate authority, such as VeriSign. Most Internet browsers already have the ability to check for the presence of server certificates right now: the problem is on the server side.

A few sites already offer certificates. When you visit these sites, you see a dialog box asking you if you want to trust the certificate; if the name on the certificate doesn't match the site you're attempting to reach, you know that something is amiss, and hopefully you leave. Perhaps your target site (your bank's URL) has been hijacked. If the certificate is OK, you then save the certificate so that when you next return; your browser will know it's reached the right address. You would then log in to the site.

Web browsers can also help in the fight. Web browser toolbars like one offered by Webroot alert users by displaying the reputation of a website.

Denial of Service (DoS)

Denial-of-service attacks prevent the normal use or management of communication services, and may take the form of either a targeted attack on a particular service or a broad, incapacitating attack. For example, a network may be flooded with messages that cause a degradation of service or possibly a complete collapse if a server shuts down under abnormal loading. Another example is rapid and repeated requests to a web server, which bar legitimate access to others. Denial-of-service attacks are frequently reported for internet-connected services.

- Attacker inundates server with packets causing it to drop legitimate packets Makes service unavailable, downtime = lost revenue
- Particularly a threat for financial and e-commerce vendors
- Can be automated through botnets

Buffer Overflow attack

Application reserves adjacent memory locations (buffer) to store arguments to a function, or variable values. Attacker gives an argument too long to fit in the buffer. The application copies the whole argument, overflowing the buffer and overwriting memory space. If the conditions are "just right" this will enable to attacker to gain control over the program flow and execute arbitrary code, with the same privileges of the original application.

How to avoid Buffer Overflows?

- Use safe libraries
  - Many vulnerabilities in code are due to unsafe use of system libraries
  - An alternative is to install a kernel patch that dynamically substitutes calls to unsafe library functions for safe versions of those
- Memory address randomization

- Patch at the kernel level, changing the memory mapping, small performance penalty, by extra memory lookups (actually, extra cache lookups)
- Makes it very difficult to perform a useful buffer overflow
- Use static code analyzer to detect buffer overflows in the code

Client State Manipulation

When a user interacts with a web application, they do it indirectly through a browser. When the user clicks a button or submits a form, the browser sends a request back to the web server. Because the browser runs on a machine that can be controlled by an attacker, the application must not trust any data sent by the browser. It might seem that not trusting any user data would make it impossible to write a web application but that's not the case. If the user submits a form that says they wish to purchase an item, it's OK to trust that data. But if the submitted form also includes the price of the item, that's something that cannot be trusted.

Cookie manipulation

Because the HTTP protocol is stateless, there's no way a web server can automatically know that two requests are from the same user. For this reason, cookies were invented. When a web site includes a cookie (an arbitrary string) in a HTTP response, the browser automatically sends the cookie back to the browser on the next request. Web sites can use the cookie to save session state. Web app uses cookies to remember the identity of the logged in user. Since the cookie is stored on the client side, it's vulnerable to manipulation. The app protects the cookies from manipulation by adding a hash to it. Notwithstanding the fact that this hash isn't very good protection, you don't need to break the hash to execute an attack.

An online shopping website attack scenario

- Attacker navigates to the online order form
- He then submits his order
- He can view the page source
- Changes price in source, reloads the web page

- Browser sends request: GET /submit_order?price=0.01&pay=yes HTTP/1.1
  Hidden form variables are essentially in clear

Cross site scripting

Web pages (HTML) can embed dynamic contents (code) that can be executed on the browser. These are called client side scripting.

- JavaScript - embedded in web pages and executed inside browser
- VBScript - similar to JavaScript, only for Windows
- Java applets - small pieces of Java bytecodes that execute in browsers

Client-side scripting is powerful and flexible, and can access the following resources:

- Local files on the client-side host
- Webpage resources maintained by the browser
  - Cookies
  - Domain Object Model (DOM) objects
    - steal private information
    - control what users see
    - impersonate the user

SQL Injection

SQL injection is an attack in which malicious code is inserted into strings that are later passed to an instance of a database server for parsing and execution.

Example:

    var Shipcity;

    ShipCity = Request.form ("ShipCity");

    var sql = "select * from OrdersTable where ShipCity = '" + ShipCity + "'";

The user is prompted to enter the name of a city. If she enters Redmond, the query assembled by the script looks similar to the following:

SELECT * FROM OrdersTable WHERE ShipCity = 'Redmond'

However, assume that the user enters the following:

Redmond'; drop table OrdersTable--

In this case, the following query is assembled by the script:

SELECT * FROM OrdersTable WHERE ShipCity = 'Redmond';drop table OrdersTable--'

Mitigating SQL Injection Risks

- Validate all input
- Use type safe SQL parameters
- Use parameterized input with stored procedures
- Use parameters collection with dynamic SQL
- Filter input
- Review of code injection
- Prevent Schema & Information Leaks
- Limit Privileges on database objects
- Encrypt sensitive data
- Harden DB server and host OS

Exercise

1. (a) Write down the main objective – sometimes called the mission – of your company/organization.

   (b) List the major types of information your company/organization requires to meet its mission. Note down any areas in which the mission makes preserving the value of information difficult.

2. Suppose that, in a passive attack, an eavesdropper determined the telephone numbers that you called, but not the message content, and also determined the websites that you visited on a particular day. Compare in relative terms the intelligence value of each approach.

3. What example of a replayed message could lead to a masquerade attack?
4. How many shared keys are required for a company of 50 employees who all need to communicate securely with each other? How many shared keys would be needed if the company doubles in size?

Chapter

Cloud Computing

Chapter Goal

After studying this chapter, you should be able to:

- Learn the principles and architecture behind cloud computing
- Learn software delivery models in the cloud
- Learn open source Openstack component architecture

Introduction to Cloud Computing

The cloud is actually a bunch of computer servers that store and transmit data. These servers are very large and can hold massive amounts of data. The servers can be housed anywhere in the world. A user accesses the data through a log-in.

Cloud computing is also better described using the different models. In the context of Software as a Service, cloud computing is a style of computing where massively scalable and elastic IT-enabled capabilities are provided "as a service" to internal / external customers using internet technologies. The four popular cloud computing models are the following:

- Acquisition Model - SaaS
- Business Model – Pay per use
- Access Model – http/https
- Technology Model – Scalable, elastic, multi-tenancy, shared

Cloud computing is a model for enabling convenient, on-demand network access to a shared pool of configurable computing resources (e.g., networks, servers, storage, applications, and services) that can be rapidly provisioned and released with minimal management effort or service provider interaction. Cloud computing customers do not own the physical infrastructure. Cloud computing users avoid capital expenditure (CapEx) on hardware, software, and services when they pay a provider only for what they use. The advantages are low shared infrastructure and costs, low management overhead, and immediate access to a broad range of applications.

Characteristics of cloud computing

- Scalability - Infrastructure capacity allows for traffic spikes and minimizes delays.

- Resiliency - Cloud providers have mirrored solutions to minimize downtime in the event of a disaster. This type of resiliency can give businesses the sustainability they need during unanticipated events.

- Homogeneity - No matter which cloud provider and architecture an organization uses, an open cloud will make it easy for them to work with other groups, even if those other groups choose different providers and architectures.

- On-demand self-service - A consumer can provision computing capabilities, such as server time and network storage, as needed automatically without requiring human interaction with each service's provider.

- Broad network access- Capabilities are available over the network and accessed through standard mechanisms that promote use by heterogeneous thin or thick client platforms (e.g., mobile phones, laptops, and Tablets).

- Resource pooling - Multi-tenant model.. There is a sense of location independence in that the customer generally has no control or knowledge over the exact location of the provided resources but may be able to specify location at a higher level of abstraction (e.g., country, state, or datacenter). Examples of resources include storage, processing, memory, network bandwidth, and virtual machines.

- Rapid elasticity - Capabilities can be rapidly and elastically provisioned, in some cases automatically, to quickly scale out and rapidly released to quickly scale in. To the consumer, the capabilities available for provisioning often appear to be unlimited and can be purchased in any quantity at any time.

- Measured Service - Cloud systems automatically control and optimize resource use by leveraging a metering capability at some level of abstraction appropriate to the type of service (e.g., storage, processing, bandwidth, and active user accounts).

Components of cloud computing

Infrastructure as a Service (IaaS)

IaaS is a cloud computing model where vendor provides underlying virtualized core infrastructure such as network, storage and compute resources to you so that you can build your software using these resources. You still have a whole lot of operation work to do. You may get an operating system but you may still need to manage and configure other components.

Server Virtualization

Virtualization is a technique that transforms physical resources into one or more logical resources that can be used by end users or process applications in exactly the same way as if traditionally using the physical ones. A good example of this technique is memory management in an operating system. Virtualization is used to allow multiple processes to simultaneously access the physical memory in a secure and transparent way via the concept of virtual memory. The physical memory is mapped onto multiple virtual address spaces, one for each process. Each process uses pages from its own address space and behaves as if it owns all of the physical address space. The memory manager is responsible for the translation between the virtual and the physical space; it ensures isolation between the processes and provides an abstract way for each process to access physical memory.

History of System Virtualization

System virtualization or operating system virtualization has its origins in the time-sharing concept for mainframes, which appeared in the late 1950s. In the case of a mainframe, time-sharing meant allowing multiple users to simultaneously use its expensive resources. Time-sharing kept the mainframe busy most of the time; whenever an executing task would wait for user input, another one was scheduled. Users prepared their tasks using remote login consoles. The next task to be executed was selected among those that were ready. In this way, users on average were executing their programs faster. In 1961, the Compatible Time-Sharing System (CTSS) deployed on an IBM 709 was the first such system developed. The next step was the development of Virtual Machines (VMs). VMs were execution environments where users would run their programs and gave them the illusion of being the only user of the machine. The first such system was developed in mid 1960s on a specially modified IBM System/360 Model 30 with memory address translation capabilities. The Virtual Machine Control Program (CP) controlled the execution and time-sharing among 14 Virtual Machines, each one executing the Cambridge Monitor System (CMS). Since the first appearance of VMs almost five decades ago, virtualization in mainframes has evolved into a mature technology. It has also gained significant attention during the last decade as one of the most promising technologies for commodity machines. The key point to its resurrection has been the virtualization of the popular Intel Pentium commodity hardware by the two leading vendors in virtualization, VMware™ and XenSource(owned by Citirx)

Traditionally, each server is hosted on a separate machine. With operating system virtualization, different Virtual Machines are created that run heterogeneous operating systems. Different server applications run within each Virtual Machine.

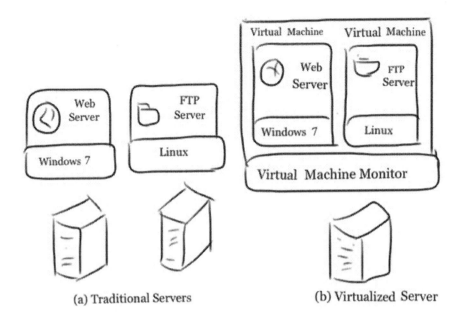

(a) Traditional Servers   (b) Virtualized Server

Sketch 9.1   Virtualized server component

Operating System Virtualization

There are three basic functionality of Operating system virtualization. Virtual Machine control, resource management and porting or migration of a VM from one machine to another. Different applications are co-located on virtualized server machines. The Virtual Machine Monitor handles resource sharing and isolation among the running applications per physical server. Applications might be distributed across several machines. The main functionality of operating system virtualization is the control of VMs. VMs can be created, paused, resumed, and deleted dynamically and on demand. Upon creation of a VM a new execution environment is created and a new operating system instance runs within it. In addition, a subset of physical resources available is allocated for the new VM. This is the equivalent of a new server machine being added to the infrastructure. The set-up of the applications running on the new VM can be either configured in advance or at run-time, exactly as it would be done as in a new server machine. One of the key functionalities offered by virtualization systems is VM resource management. When creating a VM, the amount of resources that should be made available to it is specified; that is, disk and memory space, CPU share and network bandwidth. In this way, an initial execution environment is created. This is the equivalent of specifying and configuring a server machine with specific hardware characteristics.

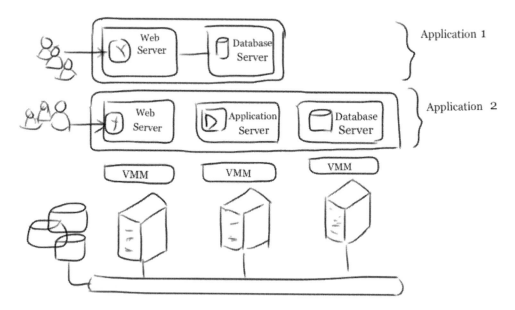

Sketch 9.2   Operating system virtualization

Platform as a Service (PaaS)

Platform as a Service (PaaS) is a software layer than can stitch together an arbitrary number of infrastructure resources (e.g. OS images, load balancers, etc.) into a single logical resource pool that can be offered to developers as a self-service computing platform. Developers and their applications are abstracted away from the underlying details of the infrastructure, relying on the application itself and common service requirements. Developers simply upload apps to a PaaS and, in a few button clicks, deploy the application. The PaaS takes care of all of the mission-critical (but strategically unimportant) heavy lifting of allocating resources, configuring the app, and deploying it to the infrastructure. All management workflows are provided by the platform and "wrapped" around applications. Additionally, a PaaS also offers platform services that an application can leverage to solve big architectural problems out of the box. A PaaS offering needs to provide applications with API access to things such as caching services, message brokering, or even application metering.

Salesforce™ platform is a good example of PaaS. It provides all the necessary components to build a customer web or mobile application. Google™ AppEngine also provides platform as a service. AppScale™ is another vendor which offers an open source implementation of Google™ AppEngine APIs so you have benefit of running it with HBase, Hyoertable or Cassandra as an underline data store. Using AppScale platform, you can run AppEngine code in your own private cloud.

IBM® Bluemix™ is the IBM open cloud platform as a service that provides mobile and web developers access to IBM software for integration, security, transaction, and other key functions, as well as software from community and business partners. Built on the Cloud Foundry open source technology, Bluemix offers more control to application developers by making service integration easy and also offering pre-built Mobile Backend as a Service (MBaaS) capabilities. The goal is to simplify the delivery of an application by providing services that are ready for immediate use and hosting capabilities to enable internal scale development. With the broad set of services and runtimes in Bluemix, the developer gains control and flexibility, and has access to various data options, from small transactional databases to large data warehouses and big data analytics.

You can use Bluemix to quickly develop applications in the most popular programming languages. You can develop mobile apps in iOS, Android, and HTML with JavaScript. For web apps, you can use languages such as Ruby, PHP, node.js, and Java™.

IBM Bluemix Architecture

Bluemix PaaS consists of applications, services, buildpacks and other components. In Bluemix, an application, or *app*, represents the artifact that a developer is building to solve a problem. The application lifecycle in the Bluemix and the Cloud Foundry are identical, regardless of how you push the application to the Bluemix. Mobile apps run outside of the Bluemix environment and use services that the mobile apps are exposed to. These services typically act in concert, and represent the back-end projection of that application. Bluemix can also host application code that the developer would rather run on a back-end server in a container-based environment. Web apps consist of all the code that is required to be run or referenced at run time. Web apps are uploaded to Bluemix to host the application.

For languages such as Java, where the source code is compiled into runtime binary files, only the binary files are required to be uploaded.

Services in Bluemix

A *service* is a cloud extension that is hosted by Bluemix. The service provides functionality that is ready-for-use by the app's running code. The predefined services provided by Bluemix include database, analytics, messaging, rules engine, push notifications for mobile apps, and elastic caching for web apps. As of writing the revision of this book, there were 50+ composable services available in the Bluemix eco system.

You can create your own services in Bluemix. These services can vary in complexity. They can be simple utilities, such as the functions you might see in a runtime library. Alternatively, they can be complex business logic that you might see in a business process modeling service or a database.

Bluemix simplifies the use of services by provisioning new instances of the service, and binding those service instances to your application. The management of the service is handled automatically by Bluemix. For all available services in Bluemix, see the catalog in the Bluemix user interface.

Boilerplates

The term boilerplate was originated from newspaper industry. Columns and other news items that were syndicated were sent out to subscribing newspapers in the form of a matrix. Once received, boiling lead was poured into the matrix to create a plate, hence name boilerplate. In computer science or programming field, boilerplate refers to sections of code which can be reused many times repeatedly without change. In Bluemix, a *boilerplate* is a container for an application and its associated runtime environment and predefined services for a particular domain. You can use a boilerplate to quickly get up and running. For example, you can select the Mobile Cloud boilerplate to host mobile and web applications and accelerate development time of server-side scripts by using the mobile app template and SDK. There are some community developed boilerplates exist in Bluemix such as Node-red starter and Internet of Things that will allow you to develop IoT applications quickly.

Runtimes

A *runtime* is the set of resources that is used to run an application. Bluemix provides runtime environments as containers for different types of applications. The runtime environments are integrated as buildpacks into Bluemix, and are automatically configured for use. Java and Ruby are some of the most popular runtimes available in Bluemix.

Buildpacks

A *buildpack* is a collection of scripts that prepare your code for execution on the target platform. A buildpack gathers the runtime and framework dependencies of an application. Then, it packages them with the application into a droplet that can be deployed to the cloud.

If you do not specify a buildpack when you deploy your application to Bluemix, built-in buildpacks are used by default.

Cloud Computing Delivery Model

Public Cloud

In a public cloud, external organizations provide the infrastructure and management required to implement the cloud. Public clouds is good at simplify implementation and are typically billed based on usage. This transfers the cost from a capital expenditure to an operational expense and can quickly be scaled to meet the organization's needs.

Public clouds have the disadvantage of hosting your data in an offsite organization outside the legal and regulatory umbrella of your organization. In addition, as most public clouds leverage a worldwide network of data centers, it is difficult to document the physical location of data at any particular moment.

Private Cloud

In a private cloud, the infrastructure for implementing the cloud is controlled completely by the company. Typically, private clouds are implemented in the own data center and managed by internal resources. This eliminates the management and security concerns associated with information being processed on third party computing resources.

Private clouds require Capital Expenditure and Operational Expenditure as well as highly skilled labor to ensure that business services can be met.

Hybrid Cloud

To meet the benefits of both approaches, you can combine public and private clouds into a unified solution. Applications with significant security level concerns for information can be directed to a private cloud. Other applications with less stringent security level requirements can use in a public cloud infrastructure.

Implementation of a hybrid model requires additional coordination between the private and public service management system. This typically involves a federated policy management tool, seamless hybrid integration, federated security, information asset management, coordinated provisioning control, and unified monitoring systems.

The two other types of cloud models are emerging lately:

Community Cloud

Cloud infrastructure shared by several organizations and supporting a specific community.

Virtual Private Cloud

Cloud services that simulate the private cloud experience in public cloud infrastructure

Classification of Cloud

Cloud can be classified based on domain and economics such as:

- Compute Cloud
- Music Cloud
- Hotel Cloud
- Restaurant Cloud

Cloud Economics – A Case Study

Washington Post: In a similar but more recent story, the Washington Post was able to convert 17,481 pages of scanned document images into a searchable database in about a day using Amazon EC2. On March 19th at 10am, Hillary Clinton's official White House schedule from 1993-2001 was released to the public as a large collection of scanned images (in PDF format, but non-searchable). Washington Post engineer Peter Harkins used 200 Amazon EC2 instances to perform OCR (Optical Character Recognition) on the scanned files to create searchable text – "I used 1,407 hours of virtual machine time for a final expense of $144.62. We consider it a successful proof of concept."

The Cloud Stack

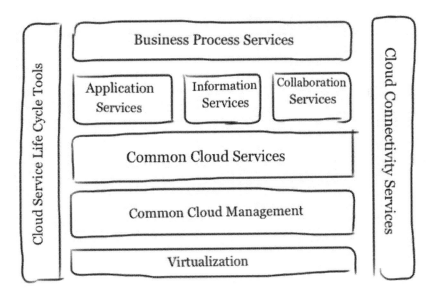

Sketch 9.3 Cloud component overview

Is your business ready for cloud?

Not every IT application, data and services are ready for cloud. Your business may be ready for the cloud if:

- the processes, applications and data are largely independent
- the points of integration are well defined
- a lower level of security will work just fine
- the core internal enterprise architecture is healthy

- the Web is the desired platform
- cost is an issue
- the applications are new

The New ACID

Old ACID –predictive and accurate

- Atomic
- Consistent
- Isolated
- Durable

New ACID –flexible and redundant

- Associative $(a \times b) \times c = a \times (b \times c)$
- Commutative $a \times b = b \times a$
- Idempotent (Idempotence is the property of certain operations in mathematics and computer science, that they can be applied multiple times without changing the result
- Distribute

Example of New ACID: Google's BigTable (Distributed Data Storage Model)

OpenStack – The open source cloud solution

"OpenStack is a collection of open source software projects that enterprises/service providers can use to setup and run their cloud compute and storage infrastructure."

— docs.openstack.org

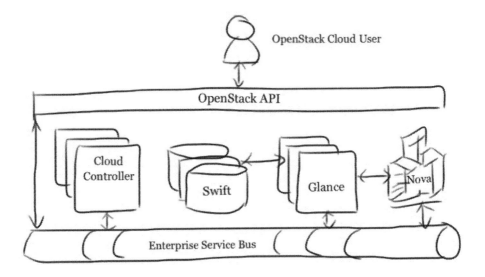

Sketch 9.4 Openstack core component architecture

OpenStack Core Components

Compute ("Nova")

- Orchestrates large networks of Virtual Machines.
- Responsible for VM instance lifecycle, network management, and user access control.

Object Storage ("Swift")

- Provides scalable, redundant, long-term storage for things like VM images, data archives, and multimedia.
- Image Service ("Glance")
- Manages VM disk images.
- Can be a stand-alone service.
- Supports private/public permissions, and can handle a variety of disk image formats.

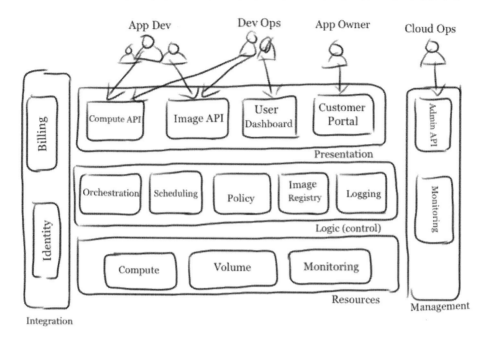

Sketch 9.5 Openstack core component architecture

As with presentation layers in more typical application architectures, components here interact with users to accept and present information. In this layer, you will find web portals to provide graphical interfaces for non-developers and API endpoints for developers. For more advanced architectures, you might find load balancing, console proxies, security and naming services present here also.

The logic tier would provide the intelligence and control functionality for our cloud. This tier would house orchestration (workflow for complex tasks), scheduling (determining mapping of jobs to resources), policy (quotas and such) , image registry (metadata about instance images), and logging (events and metering).

There will need to integration functions within the architecture. It is assumed that most service providers will already have a customer identity and billing systems. Any cloud architecture would need to integrate with these systems.

As with any complex environment, we will need a management tier to operate the environment. This should include an API to access the cloud administration features as well as some forms of monitoring. It is likely that the monitoring functionality will take the form of integration into an existing tool. While I've highlighted monitoring and an admin API for our fictional provider, in a more complete architecture you would see a vast array of operational support functions like provisioning and configuration management.

Finally, since this is a compute cloud, we will need actual compute, network and storage resources to provide to our customers. This tier provides these services, whether they be servers, network switches, network attached storage or other resources.

OpenStack Nova – Heart of OpenStack

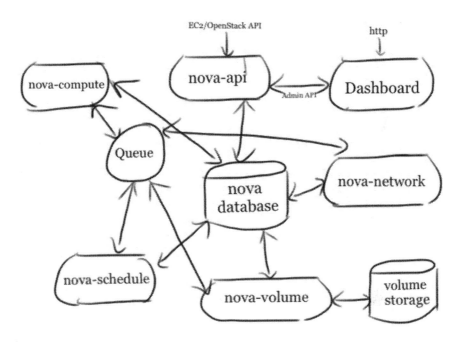

Sketch 9.6   OpenStack Nova architecture

End users (DevOps, Developers and even other OpenStack components) talk to nova-api to interface with OpenStack Nova. OpenStack Nova daemons exchange info through the queue (actions) and database (information) to carry out API requests. OpenStack Glance is basically a completely separate infrastructure which OpenStack Nova interfaces through the Glance API

Nova was contributed by NASA from the Nebula platform. Nova allows users to create, destroy, and manage virtual machines using user-supplied images.

- Corresponds to Amazon's EC2.
- Users can use OpenStack API or Amazon's EC2 API.
- Uses Python and Web Server Gateway Interface (WSGI).

OpenStack Swift

All objects stored in Swift have a URL All objects stored are replicated 3x in as-unique-as-possible zones, which can be defined as a group of drives, a node, a rack etc.

- All objects have their own metadata
- Developers interact with the object storage system through a RESTful HTTP API
- Object data can be located anywhere in the cluster
- The cluster scales by adding additional nodes – without sacrificing performance, which allows a more cost-effective linear storage expansion vs. fork-lift upgrades
- Data doesn't have to be migrated to an entirely new storage system
- New nodes can be added to the cluster without downtime
- Failed nodes and disks can be swapped out with no downtime

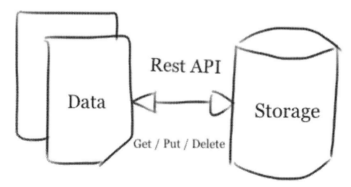

Sketch 9.7 Openstack swift architecture

OpenStack Glance

- Ability to store and retrieve virtual machine images
- Ability to store and retrieve metadata about these virtual machine images
- FUTURE: Convert a virtual machine image from one format to another

- FUTURE: Help caching proxies such as Varnish or Squid cache machine images

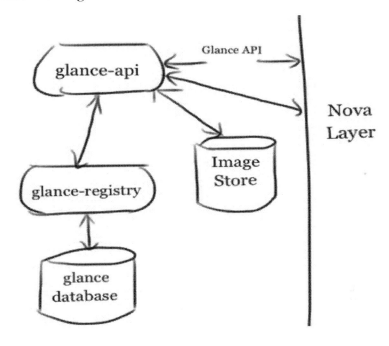

Sketch 9.7 Openstack glance architecture

Mobile and Cloud

- Number of users is enormous
- Applications become tied to "the" cloud
- Tools for building for the Mobile web
- Store personal data on the cloud (also backups.)
- Interact with situated cloud: home, car, medical….
- Mobile clouds or clouds of mobiles
- Low latency OpenFlow access to cloud via tunneling
- Elastic Execution between Mobile Device and Cloud --- thread migration and opportunistic computation

Examples

- iCloud - iOS. Music, books, apps, email, contacts, calendars, backups, apple docs.

- Google Music - Music streaming, caching
- Google Docs - Search, share, preview, view, upload, download, docs, spreadsheets, presentations, photos collections.
- Microsoft Azure – Toolkits for Apple iOS, Windows 8, Android. (Implements ICloud.)
- Pogoplug - Creates private storage cloud from your local drives, accessible anywhere.

Exercise

1. Learn the Amazon Web Service (AWS) cloud computing infrastructure hands on. Try their AWS Free tier offering at http://aws.amazon.com/

2. Research other cloud offerings such as IBM Bluemix, Force.com, and Microsoft Azure cloud and learn the technical differences in their offerings.

Project

PaaS provides application developers everything they need to quickly assemble web or mobile application using boilerplate and composable services. In this chapter project, students develop a mobile or web application in the Bluemix cloud from the project list given to them in the class.

Chapter

10

Software as a Service

Chapter Goal

After studying this chapter, you should be able to:

- Learn the characteristics of SaaS software
- Learn what SaaS means to you as a developer and an architect
- Understand the storage and security consideration in designing SaaS software

Introduction

Software as a service is a software distribution model in which applications are hosted by a vendor or service provider and made available to customers over a network, typically the Internet. The traditional model of software distribution, in which software is purchased for and installed on personal computers, is sometimes referred to as *software as a product*.

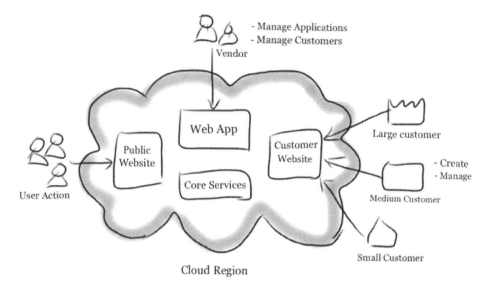

Sketch 10.1 Software as a Service architecture

What are the benefits of SaaS?

In the traditional model of software delivery, the customer acquires a license and assumes responsibility for managing the software. There is a high upfront cost associated with the purchase of the license, as well as the burden of implementation and ongoing maintenance.

ROI is often delayed considerably, and, due to the rapid pace of technological change, expensive software solutions can quickly become obsolete.

Benefits for the Users

Lower Cost of Ownership
- The software is paid when it is consumed, there is no large upfront cost for a software license since consumer does not have to spend on hardware infrastructure, installation, maintenance, and administration. For IT shop, budgeting is easy.
- The software is available immediately upon purchasing

Focus on Core Competency

- The IT saving on capital and effort allows the customer to remain focused on their core competency and utilize resources in more strategic areas.

Access Anywhere

- Users can use their applications and access their data anywhere they have an Internet connection and a computing device.
- This enhances the customer experience of the software and makes it easier for users to get work done fast

Freedom to Choose (or Better Software)

- The pay-as-you-go (PAYG) nature of SaaS enables users to select applications they wish to use and to stop using those that no longer meet their needs. Ultimately, this freedom leads to better software applications because vendors must be receptive to customer needs and wants.

New Application Types

- Since the barrier to use the software for the first time is low, it is now feasible to develop applications that may have an occasional use model. This would be impossible in the perpetual license model. If a high upfront cost were required the number of participants would be much smaller.

Faster Product Cycles

- Product releases are much more frequent, but contain fewer new features than the typical releases in the perpetual license model because the developer know the environment the software needs to run
- This new process gets bug fixes out faster and allows users to digest new features in smaller bites, which ultimately makes the users more productive than they were under the previous model.
- Additionally, it is not necessary for the customer to continually upgrade the software. Each time the user accesses the software, it is the "latest and greatest" version that's available.

Vendor Benefits

Increased Total Available Market
- Lower upfront costs and reduced infrastructure capital translate into a much larger available market for the software vendor
- Also decision maker for the purchase of a SaaS application will be at a department level rather than the enterprise level - shorter sales cycles.

Enhanced Competitive Differentiation
- The ability to deliver applications via the SaaS model enhances a software company's competitive differentiation. It also creates opportunities for new companies to compete effectively with larger vendors.
- On the other hand, software companies will face ever-increasing pressure from their competitors to move to the SaaS model.

Lower Development Costs & Quicker Time-to-Market
- The main saving is at testing (35%).
- Small and frequent releases – less to test
- Application is developed to be deployed on a specific hardware infrastructure, far less number of possible environment – less to test.

Effective Low Cost Marketing
- Between 1995 and today, buyers' habits shifted from an outbound world driven by field sales and print advertising to an inbound world driven by Internet search. The SaaS delivery model is perfect for marketing programs that exploit this shift.

Predictable MRR Revenue
- Traditionally, software companies rely on one major release every 12-18 months to fuel a revenue stream from the sale of upgrades. This puts a lot of pressure on the organization to hit an arbitrary date to meet corporate financial commitments.
- In the SaaS model the revenue is typically in the form of Monthly Recurring Revenue (MRR), which is far more predictable and less tied to the development schedule of the next release of the software.

Improved Customer Relationships
- In the traditional model once the software is sold, it is largely up to the customer to make it work. The SaaS model creates a more symbiotic relationship between vendors and customers and provides vendors with greater opportunities to please their customers

Protecting of IP
- No illegal copies
- Price is low, making getting an illegal copies totally unnecessary

What does SaaS mean to a developer?

Scale the application

- Scaling the application means maximizing concurrency and using application resources more efficiently
- optimizing locking duration, statelessness, sharing pooled resources such as threads and network connections, caching reference data
- partitioning large databases for scaling applications to a large number of users.
- Scale up and scale out

Enable multi-tenant data

- The single-tenant data models of many existing on-premise applications constrain running application instance to only use operation and business data owned by a single organization. In a multi-tenant SaaS environment, this application instance and data ownership binding must be relaxed. In order to enable multi-tenancy, the underlying application data model must be designed to accommodate flexibility for manipulating tenant specific data.
- Sharing resources (One instance to run them all)

Facilitate customization

- Many SaaS customers will want to customize the application services they subscribe to. Altering workflows, extending business documents, modifying business rules and customizing brands, logos and user interfaces are all within the plausible realms of application customizations. The challenge for the SaaS architect is to ensure that the task of customizing applications is simple and easy for the customers, yet at the same time, not incur extra manual development or operation costs for each customization. Expect meta-data to play a big part in SaaS solutions.

- Customization through configuration

Multi-tenancy

In the world of SaaS, we call subscribers of the system a "tenant"

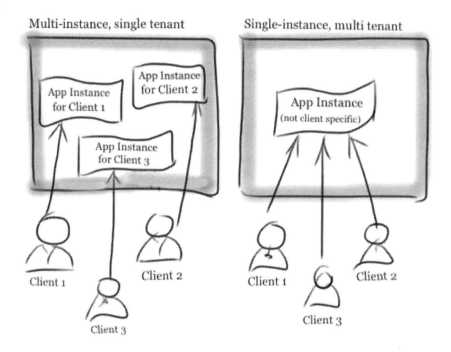

Sketch 10.2 Single Tenant vs. Multi-tenant Model

Storage Architecture Considerations – partitioning scheme

- One storage account per tenant – multiple storage accounts per subscription.
- Group multiple tenants into a storage account – enables you to group tenant by geographical region, by regulatory requirements and by replication requirements. You must still partition the data that belongs

to different tenants within a storage account using one of other partitioning scheme.

- One table per tenant – table can automatically be created in the instance provisioning process. Tenant's id is included in the table name.
- Single table with one partition key per tenant – You can have multiple partitions in a table and tenant's id is included in the partition key
- One container per tenant – this enables you to store binary large objects (BLOBs) associated with a single tenant into a container, much like a folder on a file system. This makes easy to maintain tenant specific data. For example, provisioning and de-provisioning instances, backup, archiving and setting access policies. Container creation can be automated as part of provisioning process. Tenant's id is included in the container name.

Data partitioning considerations

- One server per tenant – each database server can be hosted in different region. Vendor can put restrictions on number of databases in a server.
- One VM per tenant – tenant will have access to the database hosted in that VM
- One database per tenant – you can create one database in an each logical server or host several databases in a single server. Number of database limit will apply.
- Multiple tenants per database with per tenant tables – enable multiple tenants to share a database helps to reduce cost. You isolate tenant data by using separate tables for each tenant.
- Multiple tenants per database with shared tables – must have a partitioning scheme to identify each tenants records in each table such as using the tenant's ID as part of the key.

SaaS Security Considerations

1. The client browser sends a request to view Company 1 data.
2. The web security layer sends a request to the gatekeeper for a SAS URL that will enable read only access to Company 1 data. This data might be in table, blob, or queue storage.
3. The gatekeeper uses the storage account key to generate the SAS URL and returns it to the web layer.

4. The web layer uses the SAS URL when it queries for the Company 1 data it needs to render the web page.
5. The web role returns the page to the browser.

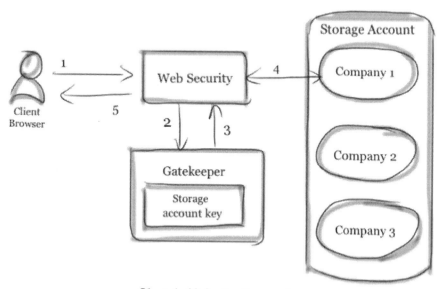

Sketch 10.3 SaaS security

Exercise

Develop a SaaS application on public cloud like IBM Bluemix, Heroku or Google app engine.

Instructions:

This exercise assumes that you have Eclipse Java development environment setup on your laptop.

1. In Eclipse, Go to Help>Eclipse Marketplace; search for Google plugin and install it.
2. Validate the plugin installation by verifying the Google Plugin in Help>About Eclipse
3. Create a Google Web Application Project from File>New>Web Application Project
4. A sample Google Web Application Project is created for you.
5. Right click on the project and run as Web Application Project.
6. Go to a browser and type "http://localhost:8888/" to launch the application deployed.

Steps to deploy the application on the Google App Engine:

1. Sign up for the App Engine Service provided by Google.
2. Register an application ID with App Engine.
3. In Eclipse, right click on the project and select Properties. Search for App Engine and enter the application ID you registered in the "Application ID" textfield within the Deployment box.
4. Go to appengine.google.com and click on your application. Copy the code and paste it in the eclipse application. Your application will then be deployed on the Google App Engine.
5. Verify the application at "<ApplicationID>.appspot.com"

You have deployed your web-app on the Google cloud ready to be used!

Chapter

11

Emerging Web Technology

Chapter Goal

After studying this chapter, you should be able to:

- Review eCommerce architecture
- Learn emerging web architecture and framework
- Apply the concept to develop responsive web application

Introduction

The number of companies carrying out business transactions (placing or receiving orders) over the Internet has increased steadily over the last decade. The Internet facilitates transactions such as ordering goods and services in two key ways. First, the Internet has increased the efficiency and lowered the costs of transactions that would have otherwise taken place offline. Second, the Internet facilitates new transactions that could not have occurred without its existence (e.g. the use of the Internet by companies to sell goods globally). Internet today generates so much economic activities that major part of economy is labeled as Internet economy. Money is made on Internet by:

- Selling goods(Amazon/Buy)
- Auction sites(eBay)
- Affiliate sites(Amazon Affiliates etc..)
- Banner Advertisements
- Group buying platform (Groupon/Google Offers)
- Portals

- Rental services
- Digital content publishing
- Online Gaming
- Online audio/video broadcasting

eCommerce and Future Supply Chain

eCommerce has flourished with the innovation in supply chain. Amazon has been leading the supply chain innovation as they have a huge stake in it. Amazon's entire business model depends on it. Big Data analytics is aiding the much needed innovation in this space. The future supply chain model will be based on multi-partner information sharing among key stakeholders – consumers (the originators of the demand signal, either from home or from a store), suppliers, manufacturers, logistics service providers and retailers.

After production the products will be shipped to collaborative warehouses in which multiple manufacturers store their products. This is a trend started to emerge as of last few years. UPS and FedEx are collaborating with the retailers and manufacturers.

Collaborative transport from the collaborative warehouse will deliver to city hubs and to regional consolidation centers.

Warehouse locations on the edge of cities will be reshaped to function as hubs where cross-docking will take place for final distribution.

Non-urban areas will have regional consolidation centers in which products will be cross-docked for final distribution.

Final distribution to stores, pick-up points and homes in urban and non-urban areas will take place via consolidated deliveries using efficient assets.

eCommerce Design Fundamentals

Create a Design That Is Built to Last and Built to Change

You might be designing a three-tier system that is to be deployed within the four walls of the company. However, a good design should allow you to extend the same solution to be hosted in the cloud without requiring a major rewrite.

- Design Incrementally and Iteratively
- Use Test-Driven Development
- Separate Your Application into Logical Units

Break your application at the user interface, business logic, infrastructure, or the data layers into distinct features that do not overlap. The main benefit of this design principle is that it allows you to test and optimize individual components without having to deal with the entire system.

Create Reusable Code Modules

Make sure that each system component is responsible for only a specific feature or functionality. Make sure that throughout the system, components are reused rather than implementing the same feature or functionality repeatedly.

Use Well-Defined Interfaces

A component should not know the internal workings of another component and should only communicate via an agreed upon interface or contract. This helps ensure that your solution is easy to maintain and extend. Typical eCommerce system architecture

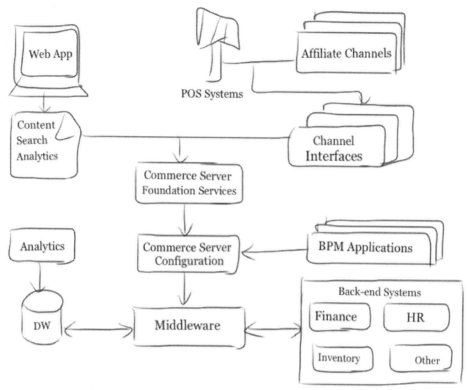

Sketch 11.1 eCommerce architecture overview

Evolution of Web Standards

- HTML – core language of the web
- W3C released RC for HTML5 (stable)
- W3C released 1st draft of HTML5.1
    - Better forms (input modes/auto complete)
    - Video captioning
    - Fast seeking
    - Spell checking
    - Better image accessibility
    - Powerful iframes
    - http://www.w3.org/html/wg/drafts/html/master/
- W3C also released Canvas2D
    - 2 dimensional graphics technology in HTML
- WHATWG
    - Unofficial collaboration of browser manufacturers and others

Responsive Web Design

Responsive Web design is **not only about adjustable screen resolutions and automatically resizable images**, but rather about a whole new way of thinking about design

#1 Adjusting screen resolution

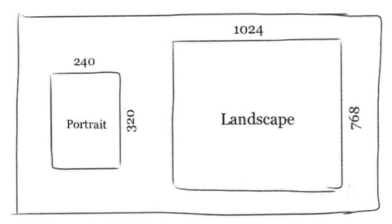

240

1024

Portrait

320

Landscape

768

Sketch 11.2 Responsive web design

#2 Creating fluid images

- Hiding and Revealing portion of images
- Creating sliding composite images
- Foreground images that scale with the layout

#3 Custom Layout structure

- Default style sheets that carry to child style sheet
- Media queries – supports new media features such as max-width, device-width, orientation

#4 Showing or hiding content

- Let's users pick and choose content
- CSS provides these options
- With the ability to easily show and hide content, rearrange layout elements and automatically resize images, form elements and more, a

design can be transformed to fit a huge variety of screen sizes and device types

Emerging Web Development Framework

Node.js

Node.js is a JavaScript runtime environment running Google Chrome's V8 engine. It is a server-side solution for java script

- Compiles JS, making it really fast
- Runs over the command line
- Designed for high concurrency without threads or new processes
- Never blocks, not even for I/O
- Uses the CommonJS framework Making it a little closer to a real OO language

What is unique about Node.js?

- JavaScript is de-facto language of client-side but node.js puts the JavaScript on server-side thus making communication between client and server happen in the same language
- Servers are normally thread based but Node.JS is "Event" based. Node.JS serves each request in an Event loop that is able to handle simultaneous requests.
- Node.JS programs are executed by V8 JavaScript engine the same one used by Google chrome browser.

How do you use Node.js?

- Node is a command line tool. You download a tarball, compile and install the source.
- It lets you Layered on top of the TCP library is a HTTP and HTTPS client/server.
- The JS is executed by the V8 JavaScript engine (the engine that makes Google Chrome so fast)
- Node provides a JavaScript API to access the network and file system.

Backbone.js

Backbone.js is a web framework created by Jeremy Ashkenas, author of the CoffeScript in 2010. Backbone.js is based on the Undersore.js library which provides many useful functions to work with arrays, collections, objects, events, and so on. Backbone.js requires jQuery

- It is minimalistic and easily integrates with other frameworks.
- It is modular, which means you can use only required functionality.
- It also has perfect OOP design and can be easily extended and overridden
- There is a growing list of Backbone.js extension

Backbone.js operates with following objects:

- Model contains data and provides business logic used in the application.
- Collection is a set of models that can be processed in the loop and supports sorting and filtering.
- View renders model or collection and interacts with the user.
- Templates are used for separation HTML from JavaSript in the View. By default Underscore template engine is used, but it can be replaced with Twig, which is used in Drupal.
- Backbone objects such as Models, Collections, Views and Router implements Event object, they can provide own events and listen to events from other objects.

Node-RED

Node-RED is a runtime and tooling on top of node.js for developing IoT applications. IoT or Internet of things is a phenomenon happening today where millions of devices around us are being connected with Internet. These interconnected devices are creating a whole new opportunity for application developers and data scientists. Node-RED allows developers to wire these devices and application flows visually in the browser. Once wired, these flows can be deployed in a run time with click of a button. Eclipse Orion (eclipse in the browser) is integrated with Node-RED which allows developers to generate java script fnctions.

You can visit http://nodered.org/ to download the tool aand start developing IoT applications.

Emerging Web Application Framework

Google Web Toolkit (GWT)

Google Web Toolkit is a powerful web application development toolkit which allows developers to create, debug/test, and run rich web applications quickly and relatively easily. It is open source, free and works in multiple IDEs as well as standalone. Eclipse is the main IDE that most GWT developers work in.

Developers can code primarily in java which is then converted into equivalent JavaScript, html, and AJAX. This makes it so the developer can focus on learning just one language instead of multiple. GWT auto-generates many of the effects such as tab-changing and pop-ups which mean you can spend more time on the logic of the application.

Application works relatively flawlessly between all browsers and the only browser specific code that you might need to write is raw javascript, css, or html which you inject yourself into the code.

Features of GWT

- One of the most advanced features of GWT is its Java-to-JavaScript compiler.
- Converts your java code to equivalent JavaScript which can then be run on all browsers.
- The compiler is extremely important is it does many optimizations of your code When you compile your program you can choose 3 different output styles. Obf, pre, or detailed.
- RPCs handle the communication between the client and the server over HTTP. They are Asynchronous. A caller can initiate a process and other processes can continue even if a response has not been received
- All objects which are transferred over the network with RPC need to be serialized.
- GWT RPC requires 3 components:
    - an interface for the service which extends RemoteService and lists all the RPC methods. This looks very similar to a C++ header
    - a class which extends RemoteServiceServlet is needed. This class implements the interface which was created above

- o Finally an asynchronous interface which is based on the original service interface needs to be defined which will be called from the client-side code.
- Since you have 3 components, it means that you'll have to modify at least 3 separate sections of your code if you want to communicate between the client and server.

Optimization features of GWT

Dead Code Elimination

It eliminates code from the output that is never called. This means, if you write five functions and only call three of them, then the compiler will ignore the other two unused functions. One benefit of this is that you can write stub functions for later use and you don't have to worry about it being generated into excess JavaScript code. It will even remove whole classes if the class is not used.

Constant Folding

If a value of an expression can be figured out at compile time, then the compiler will calculate the result and will use the value directly instead of the expression. If you write code to bring up an alert window to say 'Hello World' using concatenation such as Window.alert("Hello " + "World"), the compiler will do the concatenation at compile time and produce the following JavaScript code, $wnd.alert("Hello World")

Copy Propagation

If a variable is calculated during compile time using Constant Folding and that variable is used later on to calculate another variable, then that second variable will be calculated at compile time also and substitute the value directly. For instance, if constant folding figured out that x = 10 and later on you have y = x + 10, then 'y' will be substituted with 20.

String Interning

Saves memory and increases performance by replacing multiple references of string literals with global references.

Code In-Lining

If a called method is relatively short, it will replace the method call with the actual method.

Data Exchange on Web

"Data exchange is the process of taking data structured under a source schema and actually transforming it into data structured under a target schema, so that the target data is an accurate representation of the source data" -   Wikipedia

Popular Data exchange languages

- XML
- JSON
- YAML

Emerging Data Exchange Technology – LinkedData

Linked Data extends the original vision of the Semantic Web as being a web of interconnected links of information such as those stored in Friends of a Fried (FOAF), Resource Description Framework (RDF), Web Ontology Language (OWL) or other files.

Linked Data

- Uses URIs as names for things
- Use HTTP URIs so that people can look up those names; When someone looks up a URI, provide useful information, using the standards (RDF*,SPARQL)
- Include links to other URIs. so that they can discover more things.

Examples of Linked Data
- GoodRelations
- Schema.org
- OpenGraph

Who uses LinkedData?
- Best Buy publishes product catalog in RDF using GoodRelations vocabulary
- Facebook's Open Graph protocol uses RDF

- Google + Microsoft + Yahoo! introduced Schema.org to enable better search capabilities
- DBpedia makes Wikipedia's content available as Linked Data
- IBM Watson uses reasoning engine built on Semantic Web technology fed with information from sites such as DBpedia
- BBC uses Semantic Web technology and DBpedia to enrich BBC websites
- Cleveland Clinic uses Semantic Web technology for their Electronic Health Records to improve reporting of health care quality metrics and facilitate clinical research (study data collection, cohort identification, analysis dataset creation, etc.)
- The New York Times publishes parts of its subject headings as Linked Data
- CNET publishes parts of its product data as Linked Data on the Web
- Calais, the Thomson Reuters Web service that automatically generates semantic metadata for content, supports Linked Data for all identified entities by linking to DBpedia

Exercise

1. Nodebeginner (http://www.nodebeginner.org/) has an extensive tutorial on Node.js. Build a web application following the tutorial.
2. Create a sample TODO app using Backbone.js
3. Create a data driven responsive we application using these technologies:
   a. Twitter bootstrap as responsive UI design library
   b. SQLite as a portable small database
   c. PHP/Python as a runtime engine